MW01222911

Microsoft

Strategies and

Solutions for

CONNECTING TO

>C_u_s_t_o_m_e_r_s>>

Growing Your

Business Online

Harry Brelsford
Michael S. Toot
Karishma Kiri
Robin Van Steenburgh

PUBLISHED BY
Microsoft Press
A Division of Microsoft Corporation
One Microsoft Way
Redmond, Washington 98052-6399

Library of Congress Cataloging-in-Publication Data
Connecting to Customers / Harry Brelsford ...et al.].
     p. cm.
    Includes index.
    ISBN 0-7356-1500-4
    1. Electronic commerce--Management. 2. Business enterprises--Communication systems--Management. I. Brelsford, Harry M., 1961- II. Microsoft Corporation.

  HF5548.32 .C66 2002
  658'.054678--dc21   2001059077

Printed and bound in the United States of America.

2 3 4 5 6 7 8 9   QWT   7 6 5 4 3 2

Distributed in Canada by Penguin Books Canada Limited.

A CIP catalogue record for this book is available from the British Library.

Microsoft Press books are available through booksellers and distributors worldwide. For further information about international editions, contact your local Microsoft Corporation office or contact Microsoft Press International directly at fax (425) 936-7329. Visit our Web site at www.microsoft.com/ mspress. Send comments to *mspinput@microsoft.com*.

Acquisitions Editor: Alex Blanton
Project Editor: Sandra Haynes

Body Part No. X08-63865

Once again, my immediate family is most deserving of this dedication. That includes my wife Kristen and boys Geoffrey and Harry Jr.
—Harry Brelsford

To my mother. Thank you for all your encouragement, help, support, and love as my path winds its crazy way through life.
—Michael Toot

Contents

Foreword

Business in the twenty-first century operates under new constraints. Today, business managers must find ways to empower employees, build closer relationships with customers, and interact seamlessly with partners and suppliers. Their goals are lower costs, increased sales, and greater profits. The Microsoft Solution for Internet Business provides a comprehensive platform for meeting all of these imperatives. Created to help companies quickly design and deploy a dynamic, personalized Internet presence, the Microsoft Solution for Internet Business delivers real business value through features and functionality that increase efficiency, improve communication, streamline business processes, and help you market to customers more effectively with personalized content that can drive sales.

As the marketplace continues to evolve, organizations find that they need to work harder at anticipating their customers' and partners' needs to remain effective and maintain a competitive advantage. Initially, companies created Internet presences to display company information quickly and easily. However, customers became saturated with content and found it difficult to quickly find information that was relevant to them. At the same time, many enterprises found that the Internet could serve not only as a great communications vehicle, but also as a business channel. Conducting business over the Internet enabled companies to provide greater flexibility in dealing with their customers and partners. Although the Internet helped facilitate many purchasing decisions, many consumers were still not making these purchases on the Web. As a result, companies were not getting the type of returns on investment that they were hoping for. Additionally, while the e-commerce space was nascent, it was difficult for companies to streamline operations, improve business efficiency, and compete more effectively. Therefore, companies face two broad challenges: continuing to meet evolving customer needs while improving the bottom line.

Microsoft offers integrated solutions to solve real-world business problems using best-of-breed technology and providing enterprise-level services and support from Microsoft and its partners. Customers have recognized the agility, reliability, and flexibility that come with Microsoft products. With the Microsoft Solution Offerings, Microsoft has taken a new, more dedicated step toward addressing a variety of business needs and delivering business value. Additionally, with the help of partners and customers, Microsoft is delivering prescriptive offerings that are built on leading enterprise technologies. Microsoft is delivering specific solutions that are designed for the situations enterprise customers face today. Customers want to combine the latest technology, such as Microsoft Windows .NET Enterprise Servers, with their existing infrastructure. They want to do this quickly and cost-effectively in a way that provides them maximum flexibility to adapt and change quickly in the future as well.

Microsoft Solution Offerings are fully integrated, tested solutions that leverage the power of Microsoft products, combined with detailed architectural guidance to enable enterprises to get to market faster; deploy a solution that is reliable, scalable, flexible, and extensible; and reduce their total cost of ownership.

In *Connecting to Customers*, the authors discuss the need for and implementation of the Microsoft Solution for Internet Business from the business development manager's perspective, providing a thorough and comprehensive view of the solution from business issues through creating business value, including a benefit analysis and a deployment overview. The concepts behind the solution are explained clearly and simply so that you can take advantage of them immediately.

The Microsoft Solution for Internet Business

As the world becomes more connected, business enterprises become increasingly virtual. Enterprises need to make sure their employees are empowered, while staying at the forefront of technology for integrating with business partners and connecting to customers.

Because of the evolving nature of the Internet, companies cannot afford to allow their Internet presence to become stale. Web sites not only have to be more cutting-edge and expansive, but also more effective and continuously up-to-date. Enterprises are being increasingly pressured to create Web presences that are more focused, solve real business problems, and increase business efficiency while being effective enough to successfully compete in the global Internet economy. However, with the right solutions, companies can become smarter, take advantage of these solutions, and conduct business faster, more easily and more efficiently.

Whether bringing an existing business online or starting one anew, you need to do the following:

- Get to market fast and adapt as market conditions change
- Attract and retain customers with personalized service and a successful online presentation

- Increase sales and profitability by offering secure online shopping

- Make more effective business decisions with real-time market analyses

- Integrate and automate business processes for peak efficiency

The Microsoft Solution for Internet Business enables businesses to quickly build a dynamic, personalized Internet presence that manages relationships with customers and partners more effectively, improves customer satisfaction, provides rich online retail capabilities to expand your business, improves business efficiencies, and allows them to compete more effectively in the global Internet economy.

By focusing on the Microsoft Solution for Internet Business, *Connecting to Customers* explores such issues as empowering employees, marketing to customers more effectively in the global Internet economy, and analyzing sales data and purchasing behavior. With the Microsoft Solution for Internet Business, you can address changing customer needs to build a flexible Internet presence that can grow as your business grows.

Competing More Effectively

As companies strive to differentiate their offerings and strengthen their competitive advantage, while maintaining customer loyalty and expanding their customer base, they need to be able to provide information to their customers quickly, clearly, and easily. The Microsoft Solution for Internet Business provides numerous capabilities that enable enterprises to act on business opportunities, increase business efficiencies, and enhance customer and partner relationships. Also included are jump-start tools and enterprise-level guidance, enabling companies to build a personalized, unique Web experience specifically designed to meet the needs of their customers and partners.

Improving Customer Satisfaction

To fulfill the needs of customers and partners, sites must be effective, empowering, dynamic, and fast. Customers want information, and they want it personalized so that they can see only what is relevant to them. The majority of Internet users go online to find information that will help them get their job done or make purchase decisions. They want information personalized to their needs and interests. The Microsoft Solution for Internet Business provides personalization and dynamic content management capabilities so that organizations can provide a more meaningful Web experience. Providing this unique experience to customers helps them act on information faster and builds customer loyalty.

Getting to Market Faster

The solution enables companies to take advantage of existing skill sets and investments, reduce the development cycle, lower costs, and further accelerate the time to benefit. Additionally, the Microsoft Solution for Internet Business is a fully integrated, tested solution that dramatically reduces the integration and testing cycles required, enabling organizations to build Internet presences quickly and cost-effectively. Companies can thus focus on their core competencies and build an Internet experience that best meets the needs of their business and customers.

Establishing Credibility Through Reliability

To build credibility with customers and to truly meet their varying needs, your business needs to be able to interact with the marketplace 24 hours a day, 7 days a week, 365 days a year. As businesses grow, requirements change, and technologies evolve, these businesses must provide customers with a seamless Internet experience that continually takes advantage of new services, delivering unflinching reliability and security. The Microsoft Solution for Internet Business enables companies to further establish credibility with the marketplace by providing proven software that withstands software and hardware failures, preventing any disruption of business and potential loss of revenue. Furthermore, companies can rest easy, with the ability to perform critical operations online and conduct quicker backup operations.

In addition, the Microsoft Solution for Internet Business is built on the Windows .NET Enterprise Servers, widely recognized as industry leaders. With the solution, your business can create a secure, reliable, and scalable Web site, with complete commerce functionality and the ability to integrate with various internal or external systems.

Growing as Your Business Grows

With on-demand scalability, the Microsoft Solution for Internet Business allows an organization to scale its Web site to map very closely with ever-changing business needs. Scalability comes seamlessly, as organizations can easily add additional processors to increase performance and throughput on individual servers, using off-the-shelf PC hardware. The solution dynamically performs smart caching of your content to further ensure that you are experiencing maximum performance on your Web site.

Building a Flexible Business

To make your business presence flexible you need to scale as your business needs change, capitalize on next-generation technologies such as XML Web Services to integrate with customers and partners easily, reduce costs by leveraging existing investments, and increase your revenue opportunity by providing additional services faster. Take advantage of best-of-breed systems with the Microsoft Solution for Internet Business, which enables you to quickly and easily integrate with a variety of third-party applications and back-end systems. Additionally, your business can create a Web site that enables customers to view information and interact with your company anytime, anywhere, and on any device. The Microsoft Solution for Internet Business empowers enterprises to quickly build Internet presences that address evolving market demands, capitalize on new business opportunities, and successfully manage competitive pressures.

Empowering Your Organization

You can empower your employees by providing easy-to-use applications and tools that allow them to create, publish, and manage their own Web content efficiently without having to rely on technical resources. With workflow tools, you can ensure the accuracy of your content by facilitating content reviews with key individuals before the information is placed on the Web.

Sites must be quick to deploy and quick to change. They must be built with tools familiar to your team, and team members must properly use their skill sets. Business managers must be in control of site content and customer profiling. They must be able to make changes to content, special offers, and user profiles based on user feedback and site analysis. Web developers and designers must be in control of site usability, architecture, and design.

Increasing Revenues and Improving Sales Margins

To ensure that your business is meeting customer expectations, you can make more effective marketing campaigns and analyze customer behaviors with the most complete data capture and analysis tools available. As your business better understands customer needs, you can provide more effective merchandising, promotion, cross-selling, and up-selling techniques to grow your business and increase your revenues.

Gaining Access to New Customers

Your company can expand its reach and business capabilities by providing commerce capabilities that enable customers to purchase services and goods through a variety of channels. Build an online business and manage millions of products with easy-to-use management tools, enabling your company to remain agile and create focused strategies that grow your business more efficiently.

Comprehensive Solution, Services, and Support

You can meet the needs of your organization with a single solution. The Microsoft Solution for Internet Business was built to leverage existing investment in skill sets and technologies, to scale, to perform in mission-critical environments, and to empower the organization to achieve enterprise agility. The solution also includes industry-leading services and support to ensure that enterprises are able to meet customer and partner demands around the clock. You can quickly launch an online business with service tailored to your customers using Microsoft Solution for Internet Business.

Learning More

We invite to you learn more about the Microsoft Solution for Internet Business and how it can help your business to grow, meet the needs of your customers, improve business efficiencies, and maintain competitive advantage in the global Internet economy.

Paul Flessner
Senior Vice President
Microsoft Corporation

Acknowledgments

This book is about Internet business success stories outside Microsoft being enjoyed by real customers of Internet solutions. I hail the cooperative folks at Jelly Belly Candy Company, Gateway Computer, VersusLaw, and 101communications for providing background information to create the compelling case studies you'll read in a few moments. A tip of the hat to the Microsoft Technology Center in Mountain View, California, and an "ibid" and a "ditto" to the internal Microsoft teammates acknowledged by co-author and iron man Michael Toot.

   —Harry Brelsford

Big thank yous go out to all the folks at Microsoft who helped make this book a reality: Acquisitions Editor Alex Blanton, who kept track of all the myriad pieces that go into making a book and rode herd on us all; Project Editor Sandra Haynes, who arrived just as things got crazy and was up to speed remarkably quickly; and the Sable project team, who answered all our questions and provided helpful documents and information resources while we were writing the book. Still more thank yous go out to Karishma Kiri and Robin Van Steenburgh, who wore multiple hats as authors, editors, and technical resources in all phases of this project. Harry Brelsford gets loud cheers for his smarts, humor, business acumen, and friendship over the past several years—now take a vacation for a while, you earned it! Lastly, none of this would be possible if it weren't for my loving wife Victoria, who always knows when I need company and when I need some quiet time to think and write. I love you, hon.

   —Michael Toot

Introduction

After experiencing explosive growth and then a market correction, Internet-based businesses are once again reporting profits. This is due to factors such as the natural maturing of the Internet commerce sector over time, the refinement of business models, and the development of cost-effective, technologically robust Internet solutions. This book, *Connecting to Customers: Strategies and Solutions for Growing Your Business Online*, describes the underlying business principles for implementing profitable Internet business solutions and provides a guide to the new technologies available from Microsoft for deploying those solutions.

What This Book Is About

Internet commerce now offers compelling customer-focused products and services that are convenient to buy and profitable for a business to sell. However, few books have been written that address the current business context in which these Internet business solutions are being planned for, deployed, and maintained. Furthermore, few books present this discussion in a business context focused on profitability and success. A survey of other Internet titles shows a technical focus with little regard for the soundness of the underlying business model. *Connecting to Customers* discusses both the business context and the technical background to present a comprehensive treatment of the current state and future directions of implementing profitable Internet business solutions. Ideally, you'll find these topics are balanced to provide a well-rounded, complete, and comprehensive discussion of Internet business solutions.

Defining Internet Business

In this book, you will find a definition and an expanded discussion of what Internet business means today. At times, this definition is broad and includes discussion of macroeconomic principles, creation of wealth, and external stakeholders. Other sections define Internet business more narrowly with bottom-line calculations, such as return-on-investment (ROI) and cost recovery periods. All of these elements combine to allow you to gain insight, understanding, and perspective on what defines Internet business in the early twenty-first century.

Defining Internet Solutions

This book provides the technical foundation of past, present, and future Internet solutions so that you can relate your understanding of Internet business opportunities to the reality of capitalizing on these opportunities. While not a step-by-step guide to specific applications, this book contains a technical primer on the underlying technology that drives Internet business solutions in order to provide you with the basic knowledge necessary to critically evaluate current solutions. In addition, there are examples of Internet solutions that will help you prepare for the next generation of Internet business.

Who Should Read This Book?

If you are curious about robust Internet solutions for medium and large organizations, you will benefit from reading this book. The business principles, technical considerations, and other discussions in this book are not limited to readers interested in businesses such as the retail segment, but also apply to anyone interested in deploying Internet solutions for educational institutions, government agencies, and not-for-profit organizations.

This book was written with the business decision maker in mind—someone who wants to understand more about Internet solutions, including a broad economic view as well as detailed accounting and financial views. The audience encompasses business decision makers at different organizational levels: senior management, mid-level management, front-line management, and technical professionals.

This book can also be used to shape and broaden the business perspective of technical staff who are responsible for implementing and deploying Internet solutions, but without using the traditional step-by-step application guide approach. Rather, individuals who want to learn about the underlying technology of Internet business solutions—for example, Microsoft Certified System Engineers (MCSE)—can read this book to reinforce their current understanding and to gain new perspectives about Internet business and e-commerce.

xix

How This Book Is Organized

This book is organized into five major sections.

Part I

Part I introduces the Internet business sector. Market segments are defined, stakeholders are introduced, common themes for customer needs are presented, and broad business issues are defined. A series of real-world case studies follows, taken from both the business and governmental sectors: organizations that have successfully deployed leading-edge Internet solutions. The section ends with a look at how to improve business processes with Internet solutions.

Part II

This section introduces value-added processes as well as the flight to profitability for businesses and goal attainment for nonbusiness organizations. It also includes a detailed discussion on calculating an ROI and an extensive treatment of how to increase the value of the Internet solution (again for both business and nonbusiness organizations).

Part III

This section looks at Microsoft Internet solutions and methodologies for connecting to customers. After reading the earlier sections on the business case for deployment of effective Internet solutions, you turn to this section for more technical concepts. Topics include dynamic Web presences, Internet solutions for the retail sector, and three Microsoft solution frameworks and methodologies.

Part IV

This section describes in more detail the technical architecture of Internet solutions past, present, and future. Technology concepts are introduced on a feature-by-feature basis and explained in detail. This section is written to inform business decision makers seeking to understand the basics of an Internet solution from the technology perspective, while providing a solid introduction to the technology professional who must deploy an Internet business solution.

Appendix, Glossary

The appendix contains a case study on a firm already deploying a Microsoft Internet solution. The glossary is presented to help you understand terms and concepts that appear throughout the book.

Feedback

We count on feedback to better understand the results of our efforts. We encourage you to provide your feedback about the contents of this book by sending e-mail to any of the addresses listed below. The authors and Microsoft Press will take your feedback into account as more books in the business series are written. Thank you for both reading our book and taking the time to send feedback.

Authors

Harry Brelsford
harryb@nethealthmon.com

Michael Toot
miketo@nwlink.com

Microsoft Press

Microsoft Press provides corrections for books through the World Wide Web at:

http://www.microsoft.com/mspress/support

If you have comments, questions, or ideas regarding this book, please send them to Microsoft Press using either of the following methods:

E-mail:
mspinput@microsoft.com

Postal Mail:
Microsoft Press
Attn: *Connecting to Customers* Editor
One Microsoft Way
Redmond, WA 98052-6399

Please note that product support is not offered through these addresses.

Business Issues

Increasing infrastructure costs. Declining marginal revenues. Increasing competition from local stores, regional chains, and global marketing giants. Somehow, with all the increased pressure raising the noise to almost painful levels, you have to come up with a way to reduce costs, increase revenues, and outmarket the competition. You've been told it's a life-or-death struggle, with the life of the company at stake. Oh, and you have to have a plan ready by the end of the month. This scenario is being repeated on a daily basis in companies just like yours. If you haven't been privileged to have this discussion with your chief executive officer (CEO) and board of directors yet, chances are good you will have it before the end of your next fiscal year. What do you do?

The book you are reading was written with this scenario in mind. Using the Internet, you can connect to your customers and deliver better goods and better services, lower your hard costs, and achieve the goals set by your company's upper management. This book walks you through the business decisions involved, evaluates the financial considerations, and introduces you to a technology and services solution that will help you reach your business goals.

This first part of the book covers a needs analysis framework that helps you evaluate what your business goals are and provides you with some customer-oriented considerations that should play into your evaluation. It also looks at case studies of some companies that have faced similar issues and have built new solutions using customer-centric technology. Finally, this part reviews benefits that can be delivered by using this technology in your own business. This framework discussion gives you specific issues to think about and to present for discussion with your team, and eventually to help you make decisions and implement your plan.

Internet Solutions: A Needs Analysis

Few would disagree that the Internet has been one of the major catalysts of the late twentieth and early twenty-first centuries. New modes of communication have opened up new opportunities, methods for business, ways of connecting suppliers and customers, and ways to increase the ability to personalize communications and information depending on customer needs. This dramatic revolution is sparking customer awareness that they do not have to be bound to a single online business—that any business anywhere can provide them with the goods and services they need. Because of this new awareness, businesses are reevaluating the ways in which they connect to customers using the Internet. No longer are showrooms, salespeople, and trifold brochures sufficient to attract and retain business; instead, customers are asking for—and receiving—heightened levels of awareness, sensitivity to their needs, and customization.

Because many businesses are not equipped to deal with the "new customer," they are starting over and conducting a deep, searching reevaluation of what their customers really want and how they can deliver it. New technologies are available to help interoperate with existing systems and integrate data into new and dynamic applications that provide the highest possible level of customer service. The leading-edge companies that have done this are finding a greater level of customer loyalty, reduced marginal costs and operating expenses, and broad new business avenues to explore. It is not an easy course, but it is ultimately fulfilling for both the customer and the business.

Define the Technology and Market Segments

As the pace of technology advances increases, businesses are finding that traditional models of operation no longer provide adequate means for responding to change. This erosion occurs at all levels of business: in the way businesses deal with partners, in the way customers interact with businesses, and in the ways in which businesses operate. New demands are arising that require corporations to change the way they do business. Otherwise, they face a slow decrease in revenue and profitability as customers and competitors outflank and outperform traditional business models. Fortunately, most businesses realized the necessity for constantly improving their business models and market operations. It is not just early adopters or market iconoclasts that had this realization, but also industry pundits and traditional market leaders.

Today most businesses are looking for ways to identify, evaluate, and plan for new technologies to be integrated with their existing critical applications, business processes, and technological innovations. Despite recent economic downturns and the rethinking of existing business initiatives, most companies are looking at ways to streamline operations or enhance existing systems to regain their position in the market.

For example, International Data Corporation (IDC), an internationally recognized market survey and trends analysis company, estimates in its 2001 report, "E-Commerce Applications Market Forecast and Analysis, 2000–2005," that businesses spent more than $5 billion on e-commerce application licenses in 2000 with a projected compounded annual growth rate (CAGR) of 25.7 percent to $15.5 billion by 2005. This reflects only external spending on licenses; it does not take into account any professional services, system consulting, or integration revenue. Globally, in its 2001 bulletin "IDC's Internet Commerce Market Model: The B2B Economy Goes Global," IDC also predicts that e-commerce activity of any kind will explode from $516 billion in 2001 to $4.3 trillion in 2005. This dramatic spending level is remarkable, reflecting a strong belief among industry and business leaders that money can be made by giving the customers what they want, even if that means reinventing one's own business to do it.

Many terms are bandied about when discussing Internet-based solutions for various customer services and service integration projects. Terms like *business-to-business (B2B), business-to-consumer (B2C), enterprise resource planning (ERP), customer relationship management (CRM), supply chain-management (SCM),* and the like have been plastered in newspapers and across Web sites, heralding the "new wave" of improved business processes. The acronyms are frequently used interchangeably, and there are often contradictions between the definitions being used, even among the companies offering or selling solutions to the market in hopes of enabling online business with customers.

For example, CRM is often seen as one part of a three-pronged business process environment, as shown in Figure 1-1. CRM focuses on managing all communication and contact with a customer, whether as part of a sales call, support services, or up-sell or cross-sell marketing efforts. It is an attempt to provide a unified face to the customer and exactly the service needed by that customer at any given time.

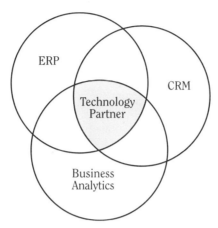

Figure 1-1. *A holistic view of how technology intersects with e-commerce–based business solutions can be divided into three categories: CRM, ERP, and business analytics, also known as business intelligence. An ideal technology partner provides solutions that intersect with all these areas when customer needs change.*

To give some examples, CRM enables business users to do the following:

- **Track customer information.** CRM systems empower business users to access, update, and monitor diverse information about customers, from simple contact information to purchasing preferences.

- **Respond to requests and anticipate needs.** CRM systems enable sales and customer support personnel to quickly respond to requests and anticipate the needs of prospects and customers.

- **Provide targeted marketing campaigns to groups of prospects and customers.** Automated targeted campaigns provide repeatable and cost-effective activities. They also enable businesses to better measure the effectiveness and return on investment (ROI) of marketing campaigns.

- **Manage customer status and activities enterprise-wide.** A key difference between CRM systems and simple contact-tracking databases is the ability to manage all phases of customer activity from prospect to postsales support. Understanding customer behavior and activities can help with customer retention, and CRM systems can help manage customer activities without increasing staff.

The complete CRM system provides tools to manage all phases of prospect, customer, and partner relationships, enabling employees to respond faster, more accurately, and more cost-effectively.

The other parts of the diagram include ERP and business analytics. ERP is sometimes seen as encompassing all B2B activity, such as SCM. This umbrella usually covers anything that involves the actual production of goods and services. As we'll see, however, this area overlaps with CRM, as B2B suppliers and customers have their own set of needs for reporting, information, and business contacts.

The third area is business analytics, or business information and reporting. This very broad area encompasses such diverse activities as data mining, financial information and reporting, and even legal compliance and logistics information not directly connected to goods and services manufacturing. Business analytics takes the information generated in the other two areas and produces reports or suggested courses of action based on transactions, market trends, external and internal data, and so forth. As Figure 1-1 shows, all these areas producing an interlocking set of business processes and activities. When evaluating your business and its connections to others, you should consider whom the different customers for your organization might be. Thus the focus is not who the customer is but what services are needed from your company. This will help you identify which methods of connecting to customers need to be changed or improved.

Identify Your Stakeholders

When contemplating new customer-focused business models, it is critical to identify both people who have the business background to understand the issues that are being faced and people who understand the technology involved. These people will be responsible for driving the customer-focused initiative and are tasked with both the authority and the responsibility to achieve corporate goals. These two groups are commonly referred to as business decision makers (BDMs) and technical decision makers (TDMs).

BDMs are commonly vice presidents of business development, sales and marketing, e-commerce and e-business, or other individuals whose primary job function is not in information technology (IT). These individuals typically have customer needs and concerns as a primary business focus and can bring valuable insight as well as direct customer connections to the table. Many of their decisions are based on information and opinions from friends and associates as well as articles in magazines or journals. Information from sales representatives or consultants ranks behind these categories as primary information sources. Systems integrators and outside consultants play a less influential role, leaving the need open for a direct relationship with technology platform providers.

Further, BDMs have a more personalized set of motivators and business relationship drivers, and most have these characteristics in common:

- Evaluate vendors for vendor contribution to achieving the key business objectives.

- Have a vendor attitude of "commitment to the BDM's business."

- Define their primary goal as personalized attention.

- Define success as delivering solutions to a BDM's individual business problems.

- Seek partners who are proactive rather than reactive in identifying issues and proposing solutions.

- Want technology to work within the framework of their existing business.

- Are very conscious of the costs and turmoil that can result from a complete systems replacement, especially for global business.

- Believe a vendor's product quality is more important than having the latest technology—it needs to work.

BDMs often become involved early in the investigation cycle, helping set a strategic direction to make sure the project is on the right track. They then become involved again toward the end of the project to help plan the project implementation and measure its success against predetermined goals.

TDMs are commonly IT directors, technology strategists, or in some cases chief information officers (CIOs). They represent a small but important segment of IT professionals. These individuals typically work within IT or management information systems (MIS) departments and, although they may wear many hats, they spend more than 25 percent of their time making strategic IT business or policy decisions.

TDMs are in the unique position of bridging the gap between a company's business requirements and the technology infrastructure that will deliver on those requirements. These individuals bring knowledge of existing infrastructure systems to the discussion and are often familiar with new or emerging technologies and how they might be used in the business. Their main areas of responsibility include the following:

- Translating an enterprise's business strategy into a technical vision.

- Defining long-term IT strategy and technical platforms for the enterprise.

- Designing the architecture for enterprise business applications.

In general, most TDMs come from a technology background, and as they advance their careers, it is increasingly important for them to not only keep current with evolving technology, but to become knowledgeable and conversant in the business implications of technology decisions as well.

Together, these two groups can address many of the questions that will arise, identify customer goals and objectives, or identify positive ways in which to reduce a customer's pain. From this group it will be important to nominate or select a champion who has the full backing and approval of the company's CEO. Many e-business initiatives fail because of a lack of full cooperation and commitment from the highest levels within the company.

With something as expansive as a customer initiative, it is likely that every group or department within a company will be affected. It is also likely that some degree of organizational change will be required, such as realigning groups or departments and merging information or data from disparate systems. Nearly every organization resists change, making the need for a champion at the highest levels who can arbitrate any disputes even more important.

This is not to say that any customer-based initiative will always be painful or disruptive to internal processes. Often, customer initiatives succeed because of the enthusiasm and creative thinking that goes into creating new and exciting ways of doing business. However, for companies that remain entrenched in traditional business models—"We've always done things this way" is their argument—there is likely to be some pain as the business is being stretched in new and unfamiliar ways.

Evaluate Common Customer Themes for Relevance

More businesses than ever are creating sophisticated new ways to connect with customers using the Internet. They're not doing this because it's the latest trend, or because they see everyone else doing it. Instead, there are sound reasons for doing this, reasons that are perceived to have short-term and long-term benefits for the company as a whole. (See *Chapter 3, "Improve Your Business Processes with Internet Solutions,"* for a discussion.) Every business has unique needs and different reasons for extending onto the Internet, but many of the needs follow common customer themes and can be grouped into a few broad categories. Some of the categories overlap, and certainly there are ones that are not included here.

Extending Business Presence Using the Internet

New or emerging businesses and traditional businesses both face a common problem: how to actively extend their business presence onto the Internet to secure increased customer revenue. New businesses have an advantage in that they are able to plan, develop, and deploy very rapidly; they have a major disadvantage in not having brand-name recognition or a large customer base. Traditional businesses have established customers, products, and services that give them a solid market presence; however, along with size comes a corporate inertia that frequently prevents the ability to plan, develop, and deploy new products and services quickly. For new businesses, the ability to conduct business online is sometimes referred to as "the new economy" or "the Internet economy." For existing businesses, this is sometimes referred to as a "brick and click" or "click and mortar" enterprise.

Both new and existing businesses want to extend their presence onto the Internet to secure new customers, new brand-name awareness, and new market segments. A static Web site isn't enough because most customers surfing the Web today are not interested in merely seeing a business on the Internet; they want to interact with it, collect information about it, and conduct business with it. As examples later in this book show, this dynamic interaction model requires repurposing many existing business systems and rethinking how to present information and business interaction technology to the customer.

Improving Customer Experience

Customers are looking for new ways to interact with businesses. They want to collect information quickly, to be able to conduct transactions, and to improve their experiences when dealing with others online. These needs can be broken down into three factors: time, convenience, and personalization.

Time is important to customers. As people's workdays and lives become busier, they seek faster, more efficient ways of conducting business: in other words, they want immediate gratification. Gone are the days when people would spend hours in line waiting for concert tickets or accept rain checks for out-of-stock products. Instead, people will go elsewhere to find someone who can provide the goods or services they want when they want them and how they want them.

Flexibility is perhaps as important as time. People turn to online sources for information about goods and services they want to purchase or to conduct business as quickly and efficiently as possible. People will read online reviews of plays or movies before purchasing a ticket, or conduct research on a car to see what other experiences people have had with a particular make and model. People balance their checkbooks, buy and sell stocks, and even play games with others over the Internet. These activities occur asynchronously; they are not likely to happen on any set schedule, but rather whenever the person has time.

Note that convenience does not necessarily obviate the need for traditional ways of doing business; rather, it can be complementary and can actually increase the ability to do business using traditional methods. For example, people might do research on cars they wish to purchase, but nothing can replace the experience of conducting a test drive. The ability to actually "try on" a car or other product will continue to be high on the list of priorities for customers. Companies that make it easy for customers to do the initial research online and then bring them to a retail store will be at an advantage compared with stores that rely solely on an online presence.

Finally, customers are interested in a customized online experience, also referred to as personalization, or the ability of a business to recognize a returning customer, remember that customer's preferences, and perhaps even provide suggestions about new goods and services that are available and that might be of interest to that customer. Personalization works much like a tailor at a high-end clothing store: The customer is greeted by name, made to feel welcome, engaged in discussion about topics of interest, and asked about satisfaction with previous garments bought at that store. New garments in the same style may be suggested, or new styles are suggested that might be of interest based on the customer's past purchasing history.

This level of personalization is fairly rare among most retail vendors, but those that use it are rewarded with a high degree of consumer loyalty to that store. Today's existing technology and tomorrow's emerging technology can provide this level of personalization to online or e-business customers and will thus provide a high degree of loyalty and return business to those companies willing to use these technologies effectively.

Reducing Costs of Securing, Servicing, and Retaining Customers

It is a common belief among business and marketing experts that it costs five times as much to secure new customers as it does to retain existing customers. It is also common knowledge that maintaining traditional service and support departments, such as banks of telephone operators, can in some cases cost as much as $75 per phone call received, regardless of the product. These two statistics show that the marginal costs associated with before-and-after sales activities can significantly eat into a company's gross receipts.

Technology provides a way to reduce those costs. Your business can reduce resale costs by using technology to provide useful and relevant information about goods and services directly to customers. Providing the ability to conduct online transactions can further reduce these expenditures. Post-sale costs can be reduced if you provide self-help and online support applications or supply newsletters or regular e-mail to customers informing them of new updates, trends, products, or other newsworthy information. By reducing overhead, it improves your ability to increase gross margins and make your company more profitable.

Leveraging Existing Infrastructure Investments

Large and medium-sized companies, and to a lesser extent small companies, have existing infrastructure investments in place that are used to run various aspects of their businesses. These systems can include inventory management, accounts payable and receivable, Web sites, e-mail, databases, file servers, and other systems necessary for day-to-day business operations. Larger companies also have applications residing on mainframes and minicomputers, many of which cannot be altered or even taken offline.

These investments in systems and applications are often extensive and expensive, and most companies have no desire to completely replace these systems, even if newer or less expensive systems promise increased savings or improved business intelligence. Therefore, it becomes necessary to interoperate with existing systems and new systems that can provide a competitive business advantage. Interoperability and extensibility are important to customers when they enable a business to respond more quickly or provide new services and products in a rapid and responsive manner. (See *Chapter 7, "Benefits Analysis: Retail"* and *Chapter 8, "Microsoft Frameworks,"* for a discussion.)

Improving Business Analytics Capabilities

As the pace of doing business increases, it is imperative to make smart business decisions based on accurate business analytics. (See *Chapter 6, "Benefits Analysis: Creating a Base Dynamic Internet Presence."*) However, many companies find themselves hamstrung by an inability to determine how their own business is doing or to answer these questions: How much in sales was completed during the past week? How much inventory is in the channel? What are the sales trends for products over a period of time? Without such knowledge it becomes difficult, if not impossible, to make sound financial and customer-focused decisions, and thus the likelihood of success diminishes.

When you consider internal employees to be "customers" you can see that they will have needs with regard to obtaining business analytics, so improving their experience online will be a priority. Your employees can use business analytics and business intelligence to help them do their jobs better and to improve your company's operations. Thus, by creating a linking mechanism that connects raw business data and applications with a presentation mechanism for your employees, you convey an immediate benefit in the form of improved efficacy and quicker, smarter business decision making.

Merging Existing Systems from Different Companies

Frequently, businesses purchase each other or merge to capitalize on complementary business strengths. However, it is extremely rare for businesses to have identical information systems or even a common method with which to exchange business data. It thus becomes necessary to build an intermediary system that can both translate and transform data for each company.

In a mergers and acquisitions situation, companies frequently set up portal sites that act as information aggregators. These aggregators contain links to information sources within each company and provide access points to departments such as human resources or IT help desks. Additionally, they can act as building blocks toward creating a more permanent information aggregation solution.

Creating a Centrally Managed Security Model

Centralized security has been a goal of IT infrastructures since the early days of networks. Companies have sought to control authentication, authorization, and access and have tried to centralize it so that all aspects of information security can be easily managed.

With businesses becoming increasingly virtualized, extending the ability to conduct business directly and with a variety of partners, it becomes necessary to likewise extend the security infrastructure. Customers want to conduct secure transactions with businesses and be assured that their transactions are both confidential and have sufficient integrity to prevent misuse or fraud. By the same token, companies want to protect business data so that customers and competitors cannot gain access to financially sensitive information or valuable trade secrets.

Customers are also aware of privacy issues, and in many cases they are refusing to conduct business with companies that sell personal information to third parties or use it in a manner not authorized by the customer. As businesses extend their presence onto the Internet, they will need to be aware of privacy issues and be able to address them sufficiently for the customer.

Create Your Plan

The phrase *connecting to customers* will mean different things to different businesses. For some, it means putting together a full-on, bells-and-whistles Web site. For others, it means creating a comprehensive self-help application that covers billing, service and support, and account management. What does it mean to your company?

Defining the Business Goal

When setting out to connect to customers you should define your company's business goals. You might be tempted to create lofty yet nebulous statements like, "Reduce the cost of doing business" or "Increase our profitability," but you should instead create more precise descriptions of what you want to accomplish. The goals should be tangible and have measurable metrics that can be used to inform and guide you and let you know when you've achieved your goal. For instance, use the phrase "will be able to" as part of the goal statement: Our customers will be able to obtain billing information and up-to-date shipping status. Our suppliers will be able to access defect reports in real time. Our news department will be able to index, search, and cross-reference all Web pages. Feel free to aim high with the goals, and don't hesitate to ask your customers and users what they would find helpful. Things you might think are not important might be at the top of the customers' lists!

Determining Limits for Your Goal

Once you have defined a goal, consider limiting its scope. Most companies plan multiphase rollouts, starting with pilot projects for select groups of users. You should approach your goal with an eye toward building some limits into the project. This will help you plan your development and deployment phases; if you set concrete, limited goals, you will have an easier time rolling out the final product to other groups.

To use the preceding examples, you could place limits like these: Our customers will be able to obtain billing information, but shipping information will have to come from a third party. Our suppliers will be able to access all defect reports, but the reports will be updated only when the batch cycle runs on the mainframe. Our news department will be able to index and search information, but cross-referencing will have to wait for a later phase. This is commonly referred to as a *gap analysis*: determining what the core capabilities of the systems are; what the company can do within a specific time period based on existing, available resources and skills; and availability of partners to help complete any gaps in the system. These limits can be seen as trade-offs from your blue-sky goals identified in the earlier step, and weighted costs should be assigned to each trade-off.

For instance, in the example of using the defect reports, it may not be possible to provide real-time reports without extensive coding and alteration of the mainframe batch process; this may not be an acceptable cost depending on code complexity, uptime requirements, application interdependencies, and so forth. The cost to implement this is high. But what if there were alternatives that could provide near to real-time reporting? Could a middle-tier application like an inventory database send an e-mail or use a messaging infrastructure to deliver a defect report? This may be an acceptable trade-off for the customer. In sum, be ready to explore why there are limitations and what those limitations are, and discuss how they affect the customer.

Drafting a Strategic Plan to Achieve Your Goal

You will need a strategic plan to act as the touchstone for all other plans and documents to follow from elsewhere in your business. The strategic plan can be thought of as a business plan: you outline what your goals are and how you expect to achieve them; the resources you can bring to bear and a list of those you need to purchase, develop, or borrow; a pro forma financial statement or list of other metrics by which success can be measured; the leadership and key participating members and a list of functions; and a description of the development and "marketing" tactics you expect to use, along with a deliverables timeline.

This is an extensive collection of information to be assembled, but use it as a guideline rather than an exhaustive checklist you need to complete. What you are looking for is enough information to get a good feeling for what it will take for your project to achieve success. Because business is moving so rapidly, you will probably not have time to complete a thorough study and have all the questions definitively answered. In fact, if you try that approach, you are guaranteed to fail as iterative document drafts make the rounds for yet another series of reviews and discussions. Try to collaborate with customers or end users as much as possible, and use their feedback as the trump card; it is difficult to disagree with what the customer wants.

The following are some questions you should answer in your strategy document:

- **Who are the customers?** Take time to identify the customers and, if possible, identify actual people or customer groups who can be contacted with questions during the development process. These people should be considered your golden resource and should be present at design meetings and key discussions about your project.

- **What are your customer's problems?** Focus on what is not working or what could be working better for the customer. Describe the problem that needs to be solved, not the solution the customer requests. For instance, don't put the solution, "Need itemized bill of materials for the product" into your document. Instead, put in the problem, "Cannot identify individual components for a product." The former is a specific implementation. The latter promotes questions: What is the user trying to do? What information about the components is being sought, and for what purpose? The responses to these answers almost certainly will surprise you and prove enormously helpful during the design and deployment phases.

- **What do the customers like or not like about your current way of doing business?** This is a series of more open-ended observations that help lend background and depth to your current project. These observations may also open up new avenues to explore with your customers. For example, if you find out they don't like your Web site but do like a competitor's, you now have an avenue to explore for new and better ways to do e-business.

- **When the project is finished, what is the expected result?** In other words, if we do this, how do we add value? Will our costs be lower because operating expenses are reduced? Will it be easier to do business with us? Will we see an increase in repeat business? You need to outline this in your plan so that your CEO feels comfortable authorizing funds to move ahead. Take inventory of your existing skills and technology investments. Determine your core competencies, and then use them as a stepping stone to help determine how you can best leverage what you already have. If you present this information to the CEO, you will be in a much better position to answer questions about why you should move forward with this plan.

Performing a Pain Analysis

The pain analysis is an important part of your strategic plan. You need to determine how much change your organization will need to endure to move ahead with your customer-focused project. What systems will you need to build or interoperate with? Will you need to realign entire departments, such as moving customer support from development to sales and marketing, or vice versa? Does this process of reaching out to customers mean you must abandon some products or product lines in favor of others? Must entire new lines be developed? All these are possible, and you need to anticipate them in your plan. After all, if you are proposing calamitous change for a net increase in revenue by 1 percent, you might need to rethink your goals, or at least put some more limitations on them.

Summary

One of the most important things to do in a changing market is to discover how best to meet customer needs. This ensures ongoing business and customer satisfaction and loyalty. New technology trends and solutions make highly customized solutions possible; it is up to each business to listen to customers, determine what solutions meet customer needs the best, and then create a plan to move forward and build those solutions. In the next chapter, you will see examples of several companies that faced increasing pressure to change the way they delivered products to customers, and how they went about analyzing the needs and designing a program to meet those needs.

Real-World Business Problems Seeking Solutions

All too often, Internet implementations such as e-commerce Web sites have been portrayed and received as solutions looking for a problem. That is, either the solution stakeholders did not focus effectively on the purpose of the implementation or the technocrats prevailed in the project paradigm, concentrating on "cool" technology instead of the underlying business purpose. These have been chronic frustrations for executives at the "C level," which include but are not limited to chief executive officers (CEOs), chief financial officers (CFOs), and chief technology officers (CTOs). However, many organizations are successfully using Internet solutions today to better connect with and embrace their customers, four of which are presented in this chapter.

In this chapter, we take a look at the elements that contributed to the successful Internet presence of four entities across four industries: two large Internet presences with more than 1000 employees—Gateway Corporation and the Internal Revenue Service (IRS)—and two medium-sized Internet presences with fewer than 1000 employees—VersusLaw and 101communications. Each of these organizations succeeded by exploiting the Internet to better connect with customers and constituents.

In the first case study, Gateway Inc., you'll see an example of how a large computer manufacturer with a branding closely tied to home computer users is tackling customer-centric Internet solution sets. Customer-centric Internet solutions are focused on the customer more than any other entity. This case study is also about "clicks and bricks," as the Gateway Web site is complementary to the Gateway Country store concept; that is, Internet customer solutions support both online and real asset operations.

The second case study, the IRS, is a stellar example of effectively connecting to its customer base (or constituency) with its Internet solution. For example, each day the IRS populates its Web site with fresh and relevant customer news relating to U.S. taxation.

The chapter then shifts to present two medium-sized businesses at which Internet customer-focused solutions are a keystone component of their respective growth strategies. VersusLaw seeks to continue its transition from a bulletin board system (BBS) to a full-service Internet provider of online legal research. It's a tricky balance as VersusLaw seeks to maintain its historical favorable profitability and compete effectively against larger competitors.

The last case study is on 101communications, a media and publishing conglomerate. This organization is using a customer-focused Internet solution to facilitate its rollout of new publications and conferences. It truly believes an existing customer is much cheaper to sell to than acquiring a new customer, as you will read later on.

These case studies weave common themes about using the Internet to solve business problems, consummate business transactions, pursue commercial opportunities, and above all, build strong relationships with customers. The case study discussion begins with a look at two large enterprises that can be classified as having a large Internet presence.

What Contributes to a Successful Internet Presence

Early Internet business successes included online legal research, payroll processing, tax preparation, and some commercial banking functions. Many of these companies benefited from the infrastructure and ease of use of the Internet. That is, a consumer seeking to verify an account balance at a bank could easily do so by making a connection from the Internet. This same consumer would gladly pay a fee to undertake this task. Increasingly, the list of Internet successes has grown to include bona fide customer interaction and personalization. This concept is explored further in the forthcoming case studies.

Early Internet failures included undertakings such as the delivery of customer services that weren't priced to cover costs, much less generate necessary and nurturing profits. Look no further than the early Internet grocery store delivery business models of WebVan and Homegrocer.com. Both started as online grocery stores that allowed customers to order food items and other staples over the Internet. These goods were then delivered to the customers' home or place of business. The two firms, which ultimately merged in an attempt to stave off business failure, were bedeviled by low customer acceptance and higher-than-anticipated operating costs. All told, an idea that looked great as a business plan didn't reach the critical mass of customers to become successful.

In the sections thaqt follow, we take a look at examples of four businesses that made a successful customer connection using the Internet.

Large Internet Presence

In this section, we look a little more closely at how a couple of large entities created a successful Internet presence.

Retail: Gateway Inc.

As far as Gateway is concerned, it's all about relationships and always has been. Founded in 1985, Gateway has grown from a two-person startup in an Iowa farmhouse to a Fortune 250 company. The company takes great pride in its personal focus, which today is increasing based on its Internet customer connection. An American success story by any measure, Chairman and CEO Ted Waitt started Gateway on his family's cattle farm and took it public in December 1993. The company, which is headquartered in San Diego, California, operates sales and technical support centers and manufacturing facilities across the United States. With respect to its product lines and services, Gateway was a pioneer in the build-to-order PC business and has expanded to offer a broad range of communications, applications, learning, financing, and computer-related services.

During most of the 1990s, Gateway seemed content to sell to families but not businesses, and it was successful with this strategy. But as Gateway wanted to move into the business market, it adopted an approach combining business bricks with Internet clicks, believing that this tactic was its best bet to compete effectively.

Beginning in late 1996, Gateway rolled out more than 300 Gateway Country stores, which complemented online ordering capability from its Web site. These initiatives have helped cast the company as a progressive leader in running a click-and-mortar enterprise while listening to and staying focused on its customers.

Gateway Country Stores

The Gateway Country store concept has served Gateway very well. Typically located on the outskirts of major metropolitan areas as well as in smaller markets, these 2000- to 5000-square-foot stores (see Figure 2-1) have provided Gateway the reach to interact directly with its business customers. The timing of Gateway's rollout of its new stores was key because, in an era of razor-thin to nonexistent margins on hardware sales and the outright downturn (as of late 2001) in the aggregate demand for PCs and server machines, it would be very expensive for others to replicate the Gateway Country store approach.

That's because the discretionary capital funds required for such a large-scale store rollout effort are harder to come by in this era of relative financial austerity, as compared to the availability of such funds in the boom time of the late 1990s, when Gateway began investing in its stores.

Figure 2-1.   *Typical Gateway Country store.*

Another key strategy in the Gateway Country store business model is a zero-inventory policy. Rather than being saddled with undesirable and expensive cost-of-funds components such as inventory purchases, storage, and write-downs, these stores carry no inventory. In a friendly and consultative manner, the Gateway business solution advisors (BSAs) meet and greet customers who walk into the store seeking computer purchasing advice. This activity typically leads to a customer order that is entered into an ordering system that in many ways parallels the Web-based computer purchasing system. Later, customers can either pick up the computer system at the store (creating another contact opportunity for the BSA) or have the system delivered to their place of business or home.

Web Site

Gateway also has a secure and sophisticated Web store. Customers can select from suggested computer configurations or create their own custom solution. Customer information and payments are handled in a secure manner. The

Gateway site is set up so that an interested customer can easily perform pre-liminary research online and then visit a Gateway Country store to see live demonstrations of the computer system. This capability is not replicated by other large computer manufacturers or even big-box electronic retailers (which depend much more on high-volume sales of goods from numerous manufacturers). This concept of a Web site plus a physical store embodied by Gateway is central to the click-and-mortar customer connection that so many businesses are seeking from their Internet solutions.

Customer Focus

There are two other ways that Gateway has extended its customer relationship by capitalizing on contributions from both the Gateway Country stores and its Web site. The first contribution is computer consulting services. Gateway works closely with key partners at each of its Gateway Country stores to provide customer-focused computer consulting services. In this context, *customer-focused* means providing an hour free initially to assess the customer's needs at the business location or to follow up on the purchase and implementation of a system. The key point is that these partners, known as network solution providers (NSPs), aren't utilized as much for their technical know-how as their customer communication skills. This consulting service delivery is consistent with the small business and household focus at Gateway. Information about and ability to procure these consulting services can be accomplished at both the stores and the Web site.

Each Gateway Country store offers training in a dedicated customer train-ing lab. Courses on computer systems, operating systems, and applications are delivered by a Gateway instructor. Here again, Gateway has created another linkage in its physical training apparatus back to its Web site. Customers can peruse the Web site to gather detailed information about training courses, including content, costs, and schedules. The same customer can also elect to take advantage of online training opportunities offered by Gateway. Practically speaking, the customer can take a combination approach, electing to attend some training courses in person and completing some training online.

Gateway and Internet Integration

Gateway's business strategy vis-à-vis Internet solutions that create customer connections play out in several ways, including those covered in the following sections.

Complete Internet Solution Set

Several opportunities to effectively exploit many of the Internet solutions features first presented in *Chapter 1, "Internet Solutions: A Needs Analysis,"* are being employed by Gateway. The Gateway branding is extended by its online presence. The Gateway Web site presents its computer products in the following intuitive selection categories:

- Home and Home Office
- Small and Midsize Businesses
- Large Businesses
- Education
- Government

Each of these selection categories then branch to selections based on specific computer products including desktops, servers, notebooks, services, wireless labs, and so on. What is really occurring here is personalization. In two mouse clicks, customers can select their customer category (for example, education) and their purchase need (for example, server) and effectively personalize their Web content. That's because the customer has provided important profile information to the Gateway Web site, allowing pertinent shopping information to be displayed fitting this customer classification (education and servers, for example). That is, several suggested solutions are presented on the Web page being viewed by the customer. In this example of an educational institution seeking a server, the customer will see the least expensive server at the top of the screen. Moving down the screen, server capabilities and pricing increase. Each of the selections can be purchased as is, compared, or customized. To compare different server models in a side-by-side fashion, the user can click Compare and select from two to four servers for comparison. This comparison capability allows customers to engage in their own research to make the best possible purchase decision.

To customize a suggested server model, the customer clicks the brand link (Gateway 6400 Series Servers, for example) on the Web page, and then clicks the Customize link. The customer could then change the amount of RAM, hard disk space, disk subsystem, and add-ons (such as a tape backup drive). This configuration can then be saved in two ways. For immediate use, the server configuration can be added to the shopping cart (Add To Cart link), which is discussed in a moment. For future use, the server configuration can be saved as a quote by clicking the Save Quote link. Both the Add To Cart and Save Quote links require the customer to provide additional profile information such as name, logon name, address, password, and so on.

The shopping cart capability is the transaction support mechanism for the Gateway Web site. It is here that a customer, after providing the prerequisite profile information just mentioned, can present a method of payment such as a credit card. Once the method of payment is accepted by the Gateway Web site, the transaction can be completed, the product order submitted to the Gateway fulfillment organization, and the product delivered to the customer.

A successful Internet presence for Gateway is all about positive customer experiences, reduced operating costs (including inventory, which is discussed next), and efficiently leveraged capital investments. Gateway, in its efforts to minimize inventory costs with the Gateway Country store zero-inventory model, seeks to accomplish the same financial goal with its Web operations. Ideally, inventory should only be held for a matter of days. In a perfect world, Gateway would seek to use its Web technology to allow it to achieve perfection in inventory efficiency and only hold inventory for a couple of hours.

With respect to the relationship between the Gateway Country stores and the Web site, there is clearly a case of cross-selling occurring here. This is in no small part because Gateway understands its customers better based on Web customer pattern analysis (that is, what customers view and purchase) and feedback from the stores. The stores sell the Web site and the Web site sells the store, a process known as *cross-selling*, which is the focus of many business decision makers at the tactical level of an organization. A customer in the store may use the Web site for future purchases and vice versa.

Typical Customer Experience

Gateway customers have a positive affinity for the firm because the customer experience is enhanced by the ability to both do business online and visit a Gateway Country store. The following is an example of one satisfied customer's experience.

After seeing a Gateway television ad for the latest Microsoft operating system in which a cow is having a conversation with the company founder, a small business customer visits *www.gateway.com*. At the Gateway Web site, the customer performs preliminary research on products and services and learns that a Gateway Country store is located nearby. The customer, whose interest is piqued by the Gateway Web site, then visits the stores, confirms his or her research with the in-store BSA, attends a training course on a new operating system, and purchases several personal computers and a server machine. A Gateway NSP, who is basically a technology consultant, arrives at the small business site with the new computer system and installs it. After the initial installation, the NSP makes periodic visits to the customer's office to perform additional work. This represents an end-to-end solution for the customer, incorporating both brick and click components. What has occurred here, simply stated, is that a potential customer initially performed Web-based research on the Gateway Web site and ultimately became a buyer, a behavior that underscores the value of customer-centric Web sites.

For customers in regions without Gateway Country stores, such as Hawaii, the Internet offers a convenient and secure way to transact business. In effect, the Gateway Web site acts as a virtual store in regions that have no Gateway retail store presence.

Government: Internal Revenue Service

Government entities use comprehensive Internet solutions to communicate a wealth of information to their constituencies using their Web portal sites. One government agency that is especially effective at the Web-based delivery of both historic and current information in the United States is the IRS. In this section, we present the IRS and its Internet solution. This includes the daily newspaper paradigm the main Web page uses, the rich content provided on the site, the ability for customers to receive information in a newsletter (push format), and the opportunity to make tax payments online.

The IRS Web site (*www.irs.gov*) stands out for its daily newspaper main Web page and its depth of historic information such as tax forms and tax regulations, which falls into the content management realm. The ability of the IRS, an organization at the short end of many jokes about slow-moving bureaucracy, to provide a relevant daily newspaper interface to its constituents speaks positively to the ease of its content management delivery system and its approval process. On the content management side, there is the demonstrated ability to update content easily and consistently. IRS content is presented in an easy-to-read, almost humorous way. It's a striking contrast to the less-than-friendly reputation that the business community generally ascribes to the IRS. In fact, the fresh daily content is nothing short of disarming and reflects a more caring organization and ultimately a more positive customer experience. This daily freshness factor is also a compliment to the internal Web content approval process occurring at the IRS. If the alleged multistep endless approval cycle that the IRS is both rightfully and wrongfully blamed for in the real world were at work with respect to "The Digital Daily" (the IRS main Web page), it would be impossible for this Web site to function in a meaningful way. Clearly, the daily content delivery has recast how the IRS approves the dissemination of information.

Personalization as a Key

Customer personalization at the IRS Web site is primarily a function of providing strong search and navigation capabilities. That is, customers control their own destiny when conducting tax research, often searching on keywords (for example, the word *regulation*). Depending on the type of research you are conducting, you'll see different Web pages returning different research products. For example, if your interest were in Schedule C forms, you would quickly be presented with the actual Schedule C as an Adobe Acrobat file for downloading and printing.

There is one other form of customer personalization at the IRS Web site that, in all likelihood, doesn't apply to most visitors, only those using the transaction capabilities described next (filing tax returns and making payments). Here, a customer can self-select a personal identification number (PIN) to conduct business with the IRS. This PIN, a combination of five numbers presented by the customer, is effectively an electronic signature, which allows that customer to verify his or her identity at the IRS Web site when filing tax returns.

Transaction support at the IRS Web site occurs in the following ways with its e-file program. Currently, there are four e-mail solutions through which different constituencies can electronically file tax forms:

- e-file for Individual Taxpayers
- e-file for Businesses
- e-file Partners Page
- e-file for Tax Professionals, Software Developers, and Transmitters

Each of these e-file options presents a secure transactional environment for the customer to divulge extremely confidential information and make electronic financial restitution to the IRS. Payment options over the Internet include direct debit and credit cards.

A customer can sign up using a one-step process: simply provide an e-mail address in the E-Mail Address field on the Join The Mailing List page and then click Submit. The IRS's security and privacy policy is posted at this Web page so that customers can understand how the IRS will use their e-mail address. For example, this policy states that the IRS won't collect personal information about you when you visit this site (including the specific Web pages visited or the time or day of your visit).

Finally, with respect to the IRS and its ability to connect with its constituency and interest groups, there is the ability to join its Digital Dispatch Mailing List. This is a "push" e-mail service that delivers "The Digital Daily" newsletter directly to the customer's e-mail address. The following information is contained in the e-mail:

- Important upcoming tax dates
- What's new on the IRS Web site
- Recently added tax forms and publications
- IRS news releases and special IRS announcements

The IRS also has a second e-mail service titled IRS Local Net that provides localized information for tax professionals.

Medium-Sized Internet Presence

Many successful business entities use Internet solutions to interact with smaller marketplaces. This group constitutes the medium-sized Internet presence (for example, companies with 100 to 1000 employees), two examples of which are profiled next.

Legal: VersusLaw

VersusLaw is a classic case study of a small business finding a niche, securing the financial backing of larger industry players, and growing to become a medium-sized company. Add in the fact that what was once a modem-based BBS is now a consistently profitable Internet entity, and the story gets much more interesting. Started in 1985 and now based in Redmond, Washington, VersusLaw provides the electronic distribution of legal research materials on the Internet. For a monthly subscription fee, lawyers who have opened an account with VersusLaw are able to log on and perform legal research. Other customer capabilities include account maintenance, such as varying subscription levels.

What's significant about VersusLaw is the added value it provides. VersusLaw not only provides legal documents, but also adds scope and depth to the content by appending the legal documents with insightful analysis and comments. This provides a richer legal research experience for the customer than would otherwise be obtained by looking at the source documents, such as court filings and judgments. Specifically, VersusLaw greatly benefits an attorney by allowing centralized, over-the-Internet access at any time for a reasonable cost. A large part of an attorney's work involves research, and if the research can be effective (the content is sound), efficient (the access is easy and fast), and cost-effective, the attorney and client are ultimately satisfied. VersusLaw benefits its customers by offering the following:

- **Case Law Research.** This is a searchable appellate court opinion database.

- **CFR Online/USC Online.** Subscribers may search U.S. Code and The Code of Federal Regulations online.

- **Online CLE.** This is a storefront that sells self-study continuing legal education (CLE) products. Hard-to-find credits in the area of legal ethics are a specialty.

- **LLR Malpractice Journal.** This is a subscription-based monthly publication that addresses developing liability matters in the context of legal malpractice and professional responsibilities.

- **CFR Update.** This is a "push" solution for legal professionals who want to be notified of current changes and updates to areas of interest that pertain to the Federal Register. Instead of having to research the Federal Register to learn of changes that might affect his or her skill niche, a lawyer can tell VersusLaw what areas should be proactively monitored and reported.

- **V.News News and Business Publications.** This search engine will gather business intelligence information for the subscriber. Business intelligence, based on search criteria provided by the subscriber, is mined, refined, and delivered to the subscriber.

- **U.S. Legal Forms.** Customers can use this online store to purchase and download U.S. legal forms starting at $10 per form.

- **Advanced Links—Weekly E-Mail Updates.** Customers can subscribe to free e-mail newsletters on topics including conflicts of interest, death penalty, driving while intoxicated, federal sentencing, immigration, legal malpractice, and legal sanctions.

- **Law School Program.** This online program allows law students to become VersusLaw customers for free while attending law school. This particular service allows VersusLaw to develop a customer relationship with aspiring future attorneys at a very low variable cost. Later, it is hoped these customers will become paying VersusLaw subscribers.

When subscribers log on, they may select from the applicable options. Subscribers can use only the content to which they are entitled. Customer information is securely stored in a Microsoft SQL Server database at the VersusLaw data center.

VersusLaw provides online transaction support by accepting all major credit cards through its secure server. Other payment arrangements include telephone, fax, or e-mail contacts to set up an account to be billed. Billings are automated using the interaction between Microsoft Great Plains Dynamics and Microsoft SQL Server.

Communications: 101communications

Businesses strive to make profits and accumulate wealth, and there are many ways to achieve these goals. One business, 101communications LLC, seeks to accomplish this using a growth strategy that relies heavily on its Internet solutions and its interaction with its customers. 101communications, based in Chatsworth, California, oversees more than two dozen publications and numerous conferences. Part of 101communication's modus operandi is to seize opportunities quickly when they are presented. This paradigm is consistent across many businesses, so this case study will appeal to the hearts and minds of the readership of this book. This might include launching a new Web-based magazine on a trial basis or trying out a regional conference to see what attendees' interest levels are. Central to this strategy are the 101communications Web sites, such as CertCities.com.

CertCities.com benefits from media sponsorship from the 101communications parent organization. Specifically, several 101communications magazines such as *Microsoft Certified Professional, ENTmag.com,* and *TCPmag.com* promote the CertCities.com portal with display and image advertising. This directs traffic to the Web site and allows 101communications to leverage several of its communication assets. For example, the prototype MCP TechMentor Summit conference that 101communications is test marketing receives broad organizational support from the promotional synergy delivered by its range of publications and companion conferences. It's entirely likely that a reader of *Microsoft Certified Professional Magazine* and an attendee at the long-running MCP TechMentor Conference might well attend the new MCP TechMentor Summit.

The Web page for the MCP TechMentor Summit not only delivers rich content containing conference details, but it also allows the potential attendee to register securely online at *www.techmentorsummit.com.* After providing basic registration information such as name, address, city, state, ZIP code, telephone number, and e-mail address, the attendee selects from the following four registration options:

- **Gold Passport Registration.** This is full conference registration plus the 1-day Introduction to Active Directory add-on for $1,299.

- **Silver Passport Registration.** For $999, attendees get the 3-day conference without the Introduction to Active Directory add-on.

- **Any 1-Day Registration.** Attendees can customize the conference track by selecting which day they would like to attend (for example, Tuesday) for $599.

- **Introduction to Active Directory.** This is a 1-day preconference add-on for $399.

As an additional variable, each of these options is available for an early bird discount rate if the purchase decision is made at least five weeks prior to the conference date. Depending on the attendee's selection, his or her shopping cart will reflect current charges. Payment may be made online with a major credit card. To better understand its customers, 101communications does ask for demographic information such as technology platforms currently in use and projects to be used by the attendee.

Summary

This chapter looked at how real entities are solving real problems and capitalizing on opportunities using the Internet. This information was presented in the context of large and medium-sized Internet presences by economic sector. In the case of Gateway, a combined retail store/Internet commerce site strategy is being deployed, as Gateway looks to the Internet to increase its profitability and ensure long-term wealth for its shareholders. The IRS is surprising people with its helpful Web site, which it uses to communicate with its constituency. VersusLaw, a legal research subscription service, is a model of profitability for online business operations in the medium-sized Internet presence category. 101communications is using the Web to support its test rollouts of new publications and conferences. In the next chapter, we'll take a closer look at how a business might go about implementing an Internet solution.

Improve Your Business Processes with Internet Solutions

Many businesses see the Internet as enabling electronic commerce (e-commerce) as an addition to their existing businesses. For Web-savvy businesses, e-commerce seems like merely another way of doing the same thing electronically that they've done in retail stores for years. The reality, however, is that the Internet does more than just enable e-commerce: it opens up a whole new way of operating a business by using the Internet as a transparent medium of exchange. The Internet no longer consists of Web pages with a few pictures of smiling people and attractive product shots; it is a way of linking together businesses and customers in a highly personalized, pervasive, and powerful way.

This shift to e-business, as opposed to e-commerce, affects nearly every facet of business operations. Some of the most visible ways, such as personalized content, involve customers. However, the most powerful ways, such as business analytics, are not always visible to customers. This chapter discusses some of the solutions that are possible within a business and across business boundaries, and how these solutions can improve your ability to connect to your customers.

Content Management

Today's organizations are finding new ways to interact with customers, suppliers, and trading partners. These interactions can be as simple as static Web pages or as complex as multitiered enterprise application integration initiatives. Often, the first challenge facing businesses is content management, the ability to make ever-increasing volumes of data available to customers in ways that are useful to them. This requires a sophisticated back-end solution that can retrieve unstructured or unorganized data, process it with business rules, and present it to customers.

With a content management system an organization can create and maintain a central repository for all the information created in the organization. This can range from customer-specific data such as invoices and shipping lists, to broad-ranging information such as catalogs, news feeds, image repositories, and messaging content. The content system has the ability to collect, collate, index, and organize data using a system that you design. The system can match business processes, calendar or fiscal dates, subject matter, or any other system.

An effective system also provides a means to publish the data collected, using sets of rules that you devise. Most companies use content management systems to publish Web pages for customers or Internet users; you can also use these systems for trading partners, suppliers, sales force automation, and other uses. The published content can be crafted to meet users' needs—for example, a sales force portal would have different content available than would a human resources (HR) Web page.

The content management system also provides comprehensive and powerful tools to manage the collected data and rule management system. Ideally, this system should be as automated as possible; this will help you minimize your hands-on involvement in managing your content, which is a typical IT bottleneck and a very expensive proposition in human costs. Content management includes setting up new document repositories, collecting and organizing data sets, and creating new indexes for searching the collected data. The management system should also be granular, allowing a fine degree of control over who has access to which data and who can add to or modify each repository. In the previous HR Web page example, nearly all employees will need the ability to read the company policies, handbooks, and form banks online, but only HR employees should have the ability to change any of the materials or to add or remove them from the company Web site.

Finally, there should be the ability to refresh data or update it as efficiently as possible. Some information is highly volatile, with a narrow expiration window (stock prices); other data remains current for a longer period of time or may never expire at all (census data). The ability to refresh stale data or filter out obsolete information must be built into any content management system.

Personalization

Personalization is the ability to customize the way you do business in accordance with a customer's wishes or needs. This can be as simple as recognizing a returning visitor or presenting unique information or data to the customer according to settings configured by the user. An example used in *Chapter 1, "Internet Solutions: A Needs Analysis,"* applies here: that of a high-end–clothing salesperson who recognizes you on sight; inquires about you, your family, or your business; remembers what you ordered and your measurements; and suggests new products that you may be interested in based on your previous purchasing history.

The goal with personalization is to make the customer feel like the only customer you have: in essence, they are "a customer of one." This behavior should be repeated for each and every customer who contacts your business. When you do this, you create an environment in which the customer feels special. When a customer feels that a business cares about his or her individual needs, he or she will tell others about the great service it provides. This level of attention is almost certain to guarantee return business and reduce your costs in customer retention. To do this, you must be prepared to offer an almost unprecedented degree of customized content and services in support of this goal. Otherwise, your customer will go to a competitor who can provide these kinds of personalized services.

The Three Rs of Personalization

There are three Rs in providing a basic level of personalization: recognition, recall, and reformulation. Recognition is the ability to identify a customer or potential customer using some form of token or authentication mechanism. With Web sites this can be as simple as a cookie on the user's system or, for more sophisticated sites, a user name and password. These can sometimes be handled automatically; depending on the relationship's sensitivity, certificates may be used for transactions between trading partners or supply chains, whereas retail sales may use cookies or logon mechanisms instead of requiring a certificate.

The second R is recall. Once a customer has been authenticated, his or her data and access to applications must be made available automatically. This would include access to account information such as mailing address or e-mail address and the ability to change or add information to the customer's record, such as a change of address when the customer moves. Controlling access for a customer applies here; for example, if you run a supplier auction Web site, you might charge different subscription levels for different access levels. It would defeat the purpose of your subscription tiers if any customer could access all information about any auction on your site. Thus your site must recall the appropriate access control list for each customer.

The third R is reformulation, the ability to apply a set of rules to the services and data you have available to provide customized content to a customer. This is especially used in portal-like services, where a customer sees lists of "favorites," browser panes with news bulletins or stock tickers, e-mail notifications, and Web pages with custom content relating to interaction with your business. The ability to refocus a large array of data and services into a unique, useful application helps provide users with the sense that they are indeed important to your business and that you seek a continued and valuable relationship with them.

Sophisticated Personalization Extensions

Beyond the three Rs, there are more sophisticated mechanisms for personalizing the customer experience. Two mechanisms that are coming into vogue are the ability to preserve a transaction context and data translation and transformation. Preserving transaction context refers to the act of playing "hot potato" with a customer—passing along the customer and transaction information regardless of the service being utilized.

For example, preserving a transaction occurs when a customer purchases a product but has questions about it; the question could be about an instruction manual, add-on options, troubleshooting, or trade-up products. In the context of preserving the transaction, it doesn't matter what the question is or what information is sought. What matters is that the customer's information is passed seamlessly among the resources at your company so that the customer isn't asked repeatedly for an account number, purchasing history, or product model number.

Preserving a transaction has two benefits: First, the customer sees only a "single face" for your company and isn't aware of any behind-the-scenes application interaction. Second, you do not need to replicate the information among multiple systems and applications, which makes maintenance easier.

The second mechanism for personalizing content is data translation and data transformation services. This is the ability to provide access to any information, on any device, at any time. Your average Web site is not viewable over a wireless PDA or cell phone display, but data translation and transformation services can take the Web site, convert it to a format understood by a specific device, and enable customers to access account information, place orders, check the status of orders, or monitor real-time information such as stock prices or e-mail messages. All of this can be done using real-time translation and transformation services to provide customized content to your customers.

Business Analytics

Business analytics is the ability to detect customer trends in your data by conducting deep data mining or analytical processing on customer behavior data. Customer behavior information includes information such as Web pages visited, time spent on Web pages, purchasing history, click-through activity, and so forth. To sift through this huge amount of data, the business system must be capable of tracking and logging customer behavior. This process is known as data collection or data aggregation, the first and most crucial step in performing business analytics.

Just collecting data, however, is not sufficient. Careful planning is needed before performing any data aggregation, as you must determine just what you are measuring and what trends you are looking for. For instance, using page hits as a counter of popularity tells only part of the story. Equally important is finding out what constitutes a page hit (some engines include all requests for all images on a page, thus grossly overinflating the statistics), what the referring sources are (did a popular Web site link to your page recently), the length of time spent on the page (are people quickly clicking through to get to somewhere else), and what information is presented on the page. Discovering these correlations and trends from this data is the function of data analysis. The two go together and should be designed from the outset to complement each other; if the proper data isn't being recorded and the correct analytics aren't set up, the information you collect might not make any sense.

More complex data and trend analysis is possible by integrating non–Web-based data into data derived from Internet-based contact. With the proper analytics you can determine purchasing trends by conducting data mining based on an individual's purchase history, correlating one customer's experience with other customers' purchases of the same or similar items, seeing which ad banners are in rotation and what the particular offers are, and so forth. If a particular product is heavily discounted but postsales support calls on that product are higher than other products in the line, you may be facing a negative margin on that product. If you find such a margin on a product, the discount amount might have to be adjusted or, in extreme cases, the product might have to be removed from the line. Discovering this type of trend requires sophisticated data analysis tools that can work across business systems or integrate different systems to leverage the collected data. This, in turn, enables better product marketing and allows customer-oriented businesses to gauge the success or failure of particular products or marketing campaigns with specific customer segments.

Reporting

Reporting is often viewed as a poor cousin to core business technology. When most people think of reporting they have in mind an image of reams of green-and-white paper output from mainframes or midrange systems, arranged in columns filled with data that is meaningful to someone, but usually not the person making the business decisions. A truly useful reporting system takes information from business analytics and makes it meaningful or presents it so it can be easily understood at a glance.

Most reporting systems have standard reports for common areas of inquiry: how many visitors to a Web site, how many broken Web page links, how much system uptime since the last restart. More comprehensive reporting systems allow users to quickly and easily create custom reports, or provide roll-up or drill-down analysis for managers who want to look behind the trends to see the raw data.

The key benefit of powerful, flexible reporting tools is the ability to make better business decisions that can improve a company's competitive position in the marketplace. For instance, if one brand of umbrella is selling better than another in one sales region, a timely report can generate a "buy" order from a supplier and alert the sales force to help push sales of the better umbrella. This helps provide smarter, more targeted customer contact opportunities and increases the likelihood of meeting customer needs in a timely fashion.

Common Systems Management Infrastructure

One of the scourges of older business management systems was that each had its own closed, proprietary management solution. Whether this was for content management, server or systems management, or application management, each one had a console or custom desktop application that was used to install, configure, monitor, and manage the system. With this system, every business needed at least one system "expert" who knew its subtleties and nuances. Furthermore, each application rarely had any skills or knowledge familiarity that carried over to other applications.

Enter the Internet, which brought a whole new level of management infrastructure to business operations. Businesses demanded—and got—systems that used open, publicly documented access and control methods so that all components of a customer's system could be managed as a whole. This enabled IT departments to concentrate on actually managing systems rather than learning how to manage individual systems. The new management infrastructure also enabled browser-based management of nearly all aspects of an application or server, allowing IT departments to monitor and troubleshoot systems over the Internet. It became easier to perform common tasks among all the systems in an organization and to automate both large and small tasks. This benefit had a positive side effect because it no longer required a highly skilled professional for every application; instead, it became easier for other IT staff to manage applications in the enterprise.

Modular Architecture

A system that effectively connects to customers must be flexible to adapt to changing customer needs, business models, technology and application improvements, and potential or actual global scope of the marketplace. The system's flexibility must also be balanced with powerful capabilities and simplified integration prospects. Ideally, the system should also consist of "best of breed" components that bring powerful, robust features and functionality to the table.

These systems aren't "plug and play," or even "rip and replace." Instead, they implement a customer connection system that has numerous benefits requiring up-front planning and testing before choosing a particular implementation to deploy. This means that you need to understand the potential benefits of implementing a customer connection solution and evaluate your existing systems to see where each of the benefits can be most effectively applied.

Often such a system is the product of collaboration between a business organization and its technology partners and system integrators. This generates a winning situation: the group that understands the business and its problems best (the business organization) defines the problem and solution scope, and the group that understands the technology best (technology partners and system integrators) can analyze the problem and create the solution efficaciously. The three-way synergy among the business, the technology, and the solution providers creates the foundation for an exciting, powerful new business solution.

The following list isn't comprehensive, but it is illustrative of the benefits that can be obtained by deploying a modular architecture into your existing business systems.

Application Integration

Application integration is a common buzzword in IT, and it is used in a variety of contexts. At its simplest, application integration is the linking of programs throughout an enterprise, but it is often used to mean much more. It frequently means integrating the presentation and business logic layers scattered throughout different applications on different platforms, or enhancing existing business logic in an application by extending the application's capabilities without rewriting code.

Application integration is often needed to extend existing applications because the existing systems are not capable of being modified. Application integration is needed when systems lack an easy way to add on new features or business logic through an application programming interface (API), or when the existing systems are poorly designed, such as when they mix and mingle data, business logic, and presentation layers into a single homogenous code base.

For example, a customer call center may use four or five different applications and a mixture of consoles, terminal windows, or desktop-resident code to look up a customer's order status. One application contains the customer name, e-mail address, telephone number, mailing address, shipping address, and social security number or uniform business identifier. Another application contains the customer's purchase order but indexes the records by customer number, not name. A third console-based application is used to check the shipping dock manifest, using an internally generated tracking number. A fourth application accesses the customer's financial data, such as invoices and payment history. A fifth application is a Web browser to a third-party shipping site to track the order's progress from shipper to customer.

The call center operator is required to manually re-enter customer data in several different application windows and must know how to use each of the five systems' application syntax. This can take several minutes while the operator searches for and parses through all the data to come up with the answer to a common customer question: "What's the status of my order?"

Application integration provides the means to link the programs, taking in data such as a customer name and number, and routing inputs and outputs between the programs until the answer is reached. This can be presented through a common interface, such as a Web browser, and instead of navigating four or five applications the call center operator works with only one, complete with text boxes, buttons, or drop-down lists. All the heavy lifting happens automatically behind the scenes. This confers multiple benefits to the customer and the company: the customer's wait time is significantly short-ened; call center training and education costs are lower; and, if the application is robust enough, it can be extended directly to the customer using the Inter-net and a Web browser, eliminating the need to maintain large telephone call centers to handle common customer inquiries.

Leveraging Legacy Systems and Legacy Data

Large corporations or enterprises have a valuable asset that other corporations can't match: legacy or historical data from long-term or large-scale operations. This data is invaluable and is one of the most irreplaceable assets a company has. The data might span decades, containing records of every transaction ever processed or any customer to ever contact the company, or important or trade secret business records regarding products or processes.

This data is normally secured on *legacy* systems, mainframes or midrange systems that were designed to handle huge numbers of transactions or store ter-abytes of data over the course of time. These systems often have large imaginary "Do Not Touch" signs on them: they work, they do the job, they are crucial to daily operation, and they cannot afford any downtime, especially when the value of data or transactions handled is in the tens of thousands of dollars each sec-ond. Systems administrators in the large-scale data centers often express the mantra, "If it isn't broken, don't fix it." The systems and applications can't be modified and frequently the data cannot be modified either unless accessed through a closed, proprietary application or operating system.

However, the data inside these systems has value more than just as a his-torical record. This value can be leveraged by accessing and manipulating the data outside the context of the mainframe or midrange system and using new business logic to extract additional value.

For example, it can sometimes be difficult to run daily trend analysis against host data, depending on the application being used. Mainframes might only run certain predefined reports during off hours in a batch process; defin-ing new or custom reports sometimes requires an expert in the application or operating system to set up the new report and schedule it properly. If a subset of the data was replicated off the mainframe onto a separate database, it becomes easier to generate new reports or secure real-time or near–real-time reporting capability. This makes data mining or data warehousing more affordable both in terms of rapidly responding to customer needs and trends, and internal development and deployment.

Internationalization

As the Internet connects customers with businesses, it is becoming more important to take a global perspective on the marketplace. It is no longer safe to assume that your customer base resides only within your neighborhood; instead, you should assume that an increasing proportion of visitors and potential customers are from outside what you traditionally consider to be your geographical market area. You should also realize that you can now reach more customers than those in your own region because of the Internet, whereas previously you were limited by whatever traditional media were used to advertise your business, such as newspapers, radio, or magazine ads.

This means you need to consider issues related to *internationalization*, the ability to properly display and work with languages of all types, from uni-directional ones such as French or Portuguese to bidirectional ones such as Hebrew or Thai. The bidirectional character sets require special handling both by back-end systems and by browser-based applications to function and display properly. Internationalization doesn't stop there, however; it also includes *localization*, which is the ability to present information in a customer's own language, including currency symbols, date and time, punctuation, spelling, and even idioms.

Using today's browser technology it is possible to determine the resident language and character set being used by the browser and, based on that information, present Web pages and other data to that user in that language. An automatic language selection feature is very helpful for a first guess, but it might be equally desirable to present an opportunity for the user to select the viewing language. This is extremely helpful in areas where many languages can be encountered in a relatively small geographic space (for example, Europe).

The benefit to properly handling internationalization issues is that it makes it easier for any customer, anywhere, to do business with you. Why limit your market to only a single language when you can reach so many more people?

Search Capabilities

Many customers connect to businesses to collect and compare information: presale information about a product such as specific features, price, delivery charges, or customer recommendations; postsale information such as options or add-ons, user manuals, or diagrams; or customer assistance information such as troubleshooting help, queries about the order itself, or subscriptions to mailing lists or newsletters. Other business sites feature news and information. These sites, especially news-focused ones or megacatalog online stores, need some way to make it easy for customers to find this information.

Most sites use powerful search engines that work in the background to parse and index information, and then make a search tool available for customers to enter particular search terms. This technology is more complex than it sounds; it takes some advance thought to choose which documents to search and index, to design search parameters that include or exclude specific terms, to generate the "top ten" query and search result sets for faster access, and to set up the necessary hardware and software to support these search engines. Nearly everyone has used a search engine on the Internet to find some form of information, only to be flooded with hits that number in the thousands—far too many results to be meaningful. Others have searched for information on a business Web site, only to retrieve hits that don't seem to be relevant to the query. Thus, choosing which terms (and in which context) to index can be daunting.

Using a sophisticated engine that can correlate customer information with product or service information, a business is more likely to increase a search hit's relevance, and thus increase the likelihood of customer satisfaction.

System Flexibility

To put a business spin on an old cliché, business applications expand to fill the space available for them. As business applications and content move to the Internet, they seem to require more: more server space, more bandwidth, and more raw processing power. Business managers hear a never-ending chorus from the IT department, requesting more hardware and software with which to run online business applications due to the increasing popularity of using the Internet to conduct business. This "More!" refrain will continue to be heard for the foreseeable future.

To help alleviate the constant shortage of server space, business systems today need to support both scaling up and scaling out, depending on which method is preferred by the IT department.

Scaling up involves using bigger, more powerful single-box solutions to handle increased processing and application demands. Large multiprocessor boxes that support 16 or 32 processors are not uncommon, and when coupled with 32 or 64 gigabytes of RAM, these are considered high-end, single-box solutions.

This kind of hardware arrangement has numerous advantages: there are fewer boxes to manage on the network, they tend to be top-of-the-line products from hardware vendors that support hot-swapping of components, there are no worries about network traffic or latency between boxes, and it's possible to assign applications to certain processors (processor affinity).

There are negatives to scaling up, however. The hardware is more expensive and requires expert knowledge on the part of your IT staff. Despite computer components that can be replaced without shutting down or rebooting a system, it is more likely that the system is subject to a single point of failure. There are sophisticated server room requirements to support the hardware, and applications may require re-engineering to take advantage of some of the high-end features.

Scaling out refers to the ability to use larger numbers of ordinary servers to support an application. Need more capacity? Just add another box off the shelf. This is a very appealing solution to some companies, as the initial hardware investment is smaller. Advantages to scaling out include the use of common (therefore lower cost) components, easier setup and maintenance, fewer specialized server room modifications, and easier and quicker replacement of failed hardware. In addition, the system is less likely to succumb to a single point of failure.

There are negatives to scaling out as well. Applications often require specialized clustering software and cluster-compatible hardware. Network bandwidth between boxes and cabling is much more of an issue. Server rooms run out of space very quickly, and it is more difficult to administer large numbers of servers individually.

Whatever the choice for your business, scaling up or scaling out (or a combination of the two), you should choose a modular customer contact system that supports your choice. It would be difficult to choose a system that supports scaling up and then find your budget will only support a scaling-out solution.

Robust Security Model

When customers engage with a business, they want to be assured of several things: that the transaction with the business won't be accessible to others within the business (data security), that it won't be changed somewhere during the transaction (data integrity), and that the transaction will be kept private from outside entities (data confidentiality). In addition, customers are now asking for—and receiving—assurances that their customer information or metadata regarding their transactions with the business likewise will be kept private and will not be sold or licensed to third parties.

Data Security

Data security usually refers to keeping data secure within the system during its normal operation. In other words, people working the loading dock wouldn't have access to the financial information kept about a company or information about transactions that do not directly apply to shipping and receiving. Enabling data security means having appropriate mechanisms in place to authenticate users and authorize access to services, applications, and data on the network. It can even mean controlling physical access to server rooms, backup tapes, and network routers.

From a business perspective, the authorization and authentication aspects must be robust enough to support all the disparate systems in use in a business, such as mainframe or midrange systems in addition to custom-made applications or Web-based data. The security mechanisms must also be flexible enough to adapt to rapid changes in status, such as adding or removing accounts or locking out employees who are suspended or fired.

Another requirement for a robust, flexible security system is *auditing*, the ability to monitor which applications are in use by which users, or send alerts if key accounts experience a rise in invalid logon attempts. If a transaction fails somewhere in the application chain, auditing can help trace where the breakdown occurred and identify the possible causes of failure.

Data Integrity

Data integrity provides assurances that a transaction remains unchanged from the point of origin to the last step in the transaction chain. The system you use to connect to a customer must not change the quantity of parts ordered from 10 to 10,000. Every now and again there is a story in the news about someone who receives an invoice for several million dollars' worth of electricity on their monthly bill. This is an example of data integrity gone awry. The scale of mistake in the electricity example belies a problem with data integrity, but the smaller problems that go unnoticed can do as much damage to a business. If customers discover they are routinely quoted one price on a product but charged a higher price on the invoice, they will quickly terminate doing business and probably notify the local authorities. This is the kind of bad publicity that should be avoided at all costs. Properly managing data integrity can minimize or eliminate this potential risk.

Data Confidentiality

Data confidentiality ensures that a transaction is not viewable while in transit or while being processed. When people talk about encrypting transactions within a browser, they are almost always talking about ways to provide confidentiality for the transaction. Encrypting is the most common form of providing confidentiality in an e-business system; it applies a mathematical formula to the data making it difficult to decrypt and typically can be decrypted only by the sending and receiving machines.

Using encryption for transactions can be both a blessing and a curse. There are numerous hardware and software solutions available for encrypting transactions or conversations between applications. Depending on the solution, though, there are trade-offs. The more secure it is, the more costly it is to use; long encryption key lengths take a toll on processor cycle usage, slowing down transactions. So although it might seem like a good idea to encrypt and decrypt all traffic for every customer, most businesses balance their needs and use encryption only when sensitive data is being used, such as credit card numbers or personal data.

If you are using or contemplating using encryption technology, make sure you understand your customers' needs and expectations for data confidentiality as well as the capabilities of the system you will deploy. You can strike a balance that will provide excellent confidentiality without making it seem to the customer that you are using slow or outdated technology.

Customer Privacy

Customers are becoming increasingly wary of doing business with companies that do not adequately protect their privacy. In pre-Internet days, this meant that a business kept details about any business transactions a secret. With today's volatile Internet, customers are insisting that information about them not be sold or licensed without their permission and are taking business elsewhere if they find that companies are violating this trust. Customers are insisting on a reasonable expectation of privacy in how information about them is used: they don't want their name, home address, phone number, or e-mail address—any personally identifying information—given to third parties without their express permission.

Businesses have another view, of course; many businesses generate additional revenue (at little or no cost) by selling customer lists to third parties for catalog sales or other product or service solicitations. Larger companies may share this information internally with other divisions, hoping to cross-sell or up-sell other products being offered by that company. Most businesses see this as perfectly permissible and encourage it as a way of marketing additional goods and services the customer might not be aware of, but might be interested in.

However your business model treats customer privacy, it's clear that there is a significant area of disconnect between customers conducting business with companies online. It's an area in which talking to customers and discussing expectations will be paramount in determining how your privacy policies will operate and how you will interact meaningfully with your customers.

Further, as people conduct more business over the Internet, inquiries about a business's metadata usage are also being limited by a privacy policy. The metadata in question is information about customers' behavior, habits, or patterns in contacting a business—what types of products are bought and from which manufacturer, how long the customers view pages about certain products, whether the customers complain to customer service after every purchase, and so forth. Customers are increasingly unwilling to have such metadata tied directly to them. Behavior patterns in the aggregate appear to be a permissible use, but if any of the data can be tied to a single customer, that arguably breaches a privacy policy.

This is another example of how talking to customers and discussing what data is collected and how it is used can lead to better understanding and better business dealings. A business system that helps provide these kinds of services to customers will be more desirable than one that doesn't.

How Microsoft Can Minimize Customer Pain

Microsoft is creating an advanced new generation of software that melds computing and communications in a revolutionary new way, offering every business the tools they need to transform the Web and every other aspect of the computing experience. This initiative, Microsoft .NET, enables businesses and consumers to harness technology on their terms. Microsoft .NET will allow the creation of truly distributed Web services that will integrate and collaborate with a range of complementary services to serve customers in ways that today's businesses can only dream of. Microsoft .NET will drive the next-generation Internet.

The fundamental idea behind Microsoft .NET is that the focus is shifting from individual Web sites or devices connected to the Internet to constellations of computers, devices, and services that work together to deliver broader, richer solutions. People will have control over how, when, and what information is delivered to them. Computers, devices, and services will be able to collaborate with each other to provide rich services, instead of being isolated islands where the user provides the only integration. Businesses will be able to offer their products and services in a way that lets customers seamlessly embed them in their own electronic fabric. It is a vision that extends the empowerment first offered by the PC in the 1980s.

What .NET Means for You

The .NET platform will fundamentally change the way that businesses and customers interact. By bringing employees, customers, data, and business applications into a coherent and intelligently interactive whole, .NET will allow businesses to benefit from radically increased efficiency and productivity.

To get a sense of the opportunities that .NET will provide, let's look at today's situation:

- The mechanisms by which customers can interact today with businesses over the Internet are extremely limited—generally to a keyboard and mouse for input, and a monitor for output.

- Customers must repeatedly act on information, rather than setting intelligent preferences that then automatically act on the customer's behalf.

- Data for the same customer across different applications and sites is difficult—or impossible—to automatically integrate into a single, coherent view for the customer.

- Data designed for a particular device—whether it's a PC, a pager, a cell phone, or a PDA—cannot be directly accessed from other devices. At best, it can be periodically synchronized.

.NET promises to address all these deficiencies by enabling access to business applications and customer data anywhere and from any device. In addition, .NET technologies will enable both loosely coupled and tightly coupled linking of applications in logical ways.

New Kinds of Applications, New Ways to Develop Them

These changes will arise from a new generation of applications, created and connected by today's software developers using the .NET platform, with Extensible Markup Language (XML) as an industry standard. From a technical standpoint, .NET will change the way that applications can be developed, and it will also enable the creation of whole new kinds of applications. .NET extends the ideas of both the Internet and operating systems by making the Internet itself the basis of a new operating system. Ultimately, this will allow businesses to create programs that transcend application boundaries and fully harness the connectivity of the Internet.

Businesses will thus benefit from radically increased efficiency and productivity, as .NET brings employees, customers, data, and business applications into a coherent and intelligently interactive whole. In short, .NET promises a world of business without boundaries.

The Core Components of .NET

The Microsoft .NET platform includes a comprehensive family of products, built on XML and Internet industry standards, that provide for each aspect of developing, managing, using, and experiencing XML Web services. XML Web services will become part of the Microsoft applications, tools, and servers you already use today—and will be built into new products to meet all of your business needs.

More specifically, there are three areas in which Microsoft is building the .NET family: the .NET platform, .NET products and services, and third-party .NET services.

- **Microsoft .NET platform.** The .NET platform includes .NET infrastructure and tools to build and operate a new generation of services; .NET user experience to enable rich clients; .NET building block services, a new generation of highly distributed mega-services; and .NET device software to enable a new breed of smart Internet devices.

- **Microsoft .NET products and services.** Includes Windows .NET, with a core integrated set of building block services; MSN .NET; personal subscription services; Office .NET; Visual Studio .NET; and bCentral for .NET.

- **Third-party .NET services.** A vast range of partners and developers will have the opportunity to produce corporate and vertical services built on the .NET platform.

For customers, this means the simplicity of integrated services; unified browsing, editing, and authoring; access to all files, work, and media online and offline; a holistic experience across devices; personalization everywhere; and zero management. It means, for example, that any change to customer information—whether input using a PC or handheld or smart credit card—will instantly and automatically be available everywhere that information is needed.

For businesses, it means unified browsing, editing, and authoring; rich coordinated communication; a seamless mobile experience; and powerful information-management and e-commerce tools that will transparently move between internal and Internet-based services, supporting a new era of dynamic trading relationships.

The Microsoft .NET vision means empowerment for customers, businesses, software developers, and the entire industry. It means unleashing the full potential of the Internet, and it means the Web the way the customer wants it.

Summary

A robust extension of your business onto the Internet will bring you numerous benefits, including the ability to better manage your Web content, provide a personalized experience to new and returning customers, and give you real-time or near–real-time business analytics to enable better business decisions. Microsoft's solution will bring all these benefits to you, along with industry-leading ease of use, implementation, maintenance, and open-standards architecture.

Once you understand the benefits that can be achieved for your business, you can begin planning a roadmap to achieving those benefits. The next two chapters discuss how to evaluate the return on investment that can be brought to your business and how to create value for your business using these solutions.

Business Value

Selling goods and services to customers is a privilege that must be earned every day by business, educational, and even government organizations. The ability to exist as a successful economic entity occurs because a positive return on investment (ROI) is earned in the long run. Organizations that do not earn a positive ROI in the long term have not earned the privilege of serving their customers. These are the central points in the forthcoming discussion on creating and measuring value using Internet solutions. Chapter 4 views ROI concepts from an Internet solutions perspective. Chapter 5 addresses how to create and boost ROI value in the context of Internet solutions.

New Rules for Return on Investment

All organizations have a stewardship role to prudently oversee the financial resources entrusted to them. This includes a fiduciary obligation to seek a reasonable return on investment (ROI). These two sentences might seem obvious, but they underscore and set the foundation of what this chapter and the next are about: applying traditional financial performance measures to a new field of business, Internet solutions. This results in some new thinking about ROI, including the recovery period used and how costs are measured (two specific topics addressed later). The brief explanation that follows focuses on the idea of de-emphasizing ROI in certain cases in which competitive reposition pressures warrant investigating other measures.

Note This chapter, a primer on ROI mechanics, sets up the next chapter on creating business value.

Defining Return On Investment

ROI, a standard by which all investments are measured, is really just a simple mathematical calculation based on assumptions. The ROI for any given investment opportunity is evaluated against the ROI for competing investments. All risks being equal, the business manager will invest the firm's financial resources in the investment with the best ROI. However, rarely do two investment opportunities have the same risk characteristics. At this point, the business manager must make a subjective decision about which investment inherently holds the higher risk. A riskier investment is then effectively penalized because the business manager will insist that it must have a higher ROI to offset the increased risk. Conversely, other risk-free investments (for example, government bonds) have substandard or very low rates of return as measured by ROI. Incidentally, the people who purchase government bonds are the most conservative investors or those seeking a hedge to offset risky investments.

This is the classic risk–return trade-off mechanism that is quantified by ROI. In general, investments with a higher risk need a higher ROI to attract investment capital and induce business managers to make investments. The reverse is also true: less risky investments can offer lower returns and still attract capital. The rational business manager, although attracted by higher returns, will balance the ROI with risk preferences. Some business managers have a high tolerance for risk; others do not. Many financial analysts consider the early Internet investment epoch, dating between 1995 and the end of the 1990s, to be characterized by high risk and higher anticipated ROIs on invested capital. However, the true nature of risk revealed itself, and in many cases, the adverse side of risk prevailed, resulting in low or negative rates of return to investors. As the Internet sector matures, investors are not assuming as much risk and have lowered the aggregate ROI expectations. This is a healthy trend because it brings this sector in line with the traditional business investments that yield a "normal" rate of return.

If you look back at the Gateway case study in *Chapter 2, "Real-World Business Problems Seeking Solutions,"* you can imagine an investment manager considering ROI. When faced with opening a new Gateway Country store (a traditional investment in a plant) or investing in new Web-based technology (an Internet investment), the investment manager would assess the ROI of each investment proposition. ROI is the variable that allows these "apples" and "oranges" to be compared. The steps to calculate ROI are presented after the next sections that define the ROI components.

Recovery Periods

Internet time is a frequently used term often associated with the rapid pace at which business is conducted, such as accelerated communications using instant messaging and e-mail; however, the term has financial implications with respect to ROI. Recovery periods are based on four possibilities: tax laws, physical obsolescence, management accounting decisions, and the subjective method.

Tax Laws

A taxing authority, such as the U.S. government, can often dictate how rapidly you recover your costs, and you may elect to use this value as the recovery period for your ROI calculation. For example, a rental property may be depreciated over 19 years according to one set of current tax laws (even though real estate such as rental properties historically appreciates in value). Computer equipment, including hardware and software, is often depreciated over three years. This three-year value is considered a standard recovery period for technology assets, including Internet solution deployments (the example used in this chapter assumes a three-year recovery period). However, it is possible that you will be involved in Internet solution deployments in which there might be cause to have an accelerated recovery period of 18 months or less. Chalk it up to Internet time!

Physical Obsolescence

With plant and equipment in a traditional business, including computer equipment, there is a phenomenon called *physical obsolescence*. The plant, equipment, or some other component wears to the point of uselessness or it becomes uncompetitive, often costing more to operate than is justifiable. This phenomenon could easily apply to Internet solutions technology, in which a technology implementation is obsolete within a few years. The estimated time to physical obsolescence would constitute the recovery period for an ROI calculation.

Management Accounting

More than traditional business accounting practices in the past, firms in the Internet sector are recasting earnings using pro forma methods. Pro forma accounting statements allow wide latitude in reporting special items, such as write-downs. In this accounting climate a firm might elect to treat the costs associated with an Internet solution deployment as a special item, writing off the costs against one accounting period. There may be compelling accounting reasons for doing this, but it would play havoc with an ROI calculation in which you are seeking a reasonable amount of time to earn a reasonable ROI.

Subjective

Finally, the recovery period used in an ROI calculation is often merely a subjective "guesstimate." A business manager simply selects a reasonable period of time for which the investment should be made. A common standard is to select three or five years. Durations longer than five years are often suspect because it's difficult to predict business climates and the appeal of Internet solutions for longer periods.

Measuring Costs

Calculating the costs of developing and deploying an Internet solution, a critical component in determining your ROI, is harder than it looks. This topic can be divided into hard and soft costs.

Hard Costs

The simplest costs to track are *hard costs*, which are identifiable costs for the actual services, software, and even hardware associated with the project (in this case, an Internet solution). By gathering invoices from vendors, payroll time sheets, and other source documents, you can easily calculate what has been spent on the project. For example, you might find that the software costs $55,000 and the associated hardware to run it costs $100,000. Add $100,000 in consulting fees and other identifiable costs and you would have project-related costs of $255,000 in this scenario.

Soft Costs

Deriving *soft costs* is a trickier proposition. Here, the firm might elect to allocate some overhead to the Internet solutions project. For example, if the executive team is devoting 5 percent of its attention to the Internet solutions project, a similar amount of executive overhead can be added to the project's costs. If the entire executive level spends $1 million per year on salaries, office space, and so on, in this scenario, $50,000 would be added to the Internet solutions project (this amount represents 5 percent of total executive overhead).

Soft costs allocation decisions tend to be made in a non-technical, often political, environment. The CEO might elect to allocate an unreasonably high amount of executive-level overhead to the project if he or she somehow disapproves of it. This can effectively make the project unfeasible because the ROI becomes unacceptably low as the costs grow larger.

Be aware that the internal champion of an Internet solutions project in a firm may also need to walk a fine line. The balancing act requires the realization and recognition of the true costs of the project and successfully fending off unreasonable soft cost allocations that don't speak to the project's true financial performance.

Cash Inflows

A final ROI component is the cash inflows that result from the investment. In the case of the ongoing example used in this chapter, that would be the revenues associated with the Internet solutions project. In this example, assume the increased revenues are $150,000 per year as a result of deploying the Internet solution. There can be a measurement problem in breaking out exact revenues associated with an Internet solution in a large organization. Often, a reasonable assumption will be made as to which revenues are attributable to the investment (in this case, an Internet solution).

Calculating ROI

The last few sections in this chapter have defined each ROI component for our example scenario. These are summarized in Table 4-1.

Table 4-1. Internet Solutions ROI Components

Component	Cost
Hard Costs	$255,000
Soft Costs	$50,000
Total costs (investment)	$305,000
Duration	3 years
Cash inflows (periodic inflows)	$150,000/year for 3 years

The formula for calculating ROI is ((periodic inflow × duration) – investment) / investment. Using the values in Table 4-1, the formula is (($150,000 x 3) – $305,000) / $305,000. The resulting ROI in this example is 48 percent, a respectable value.

Finally, ROI analysis is usually viewed from the perspective that each investment must carry itself. In the case of the Internet solution, it must be financially viable in its own right and not be subsidized by some other investment held by the organization.

Note   Interestingly, portfolio theory, which is not the subject of this chapter (in fact, you would need to consult an advanced finance text), does allow for some "star" investments to offset underperforming investments.

Going Beyond ROI

ROI is widely recognized as a standard measure of financial performance, but many financial professionals and MBA-types look to other financial measurements to assess the true performance of an investment. Furthermore, there are members of the business community who feel that traditional financial measurements don't apply in the Internet era. This latter view, frequently heard on 24-hour financial news cable channels, is often used to justify the significant overvaluation of Internet-based equities. Quite frankly, this latter viewpoint is based on "puffing" or inflated expectations and not sincere candor.

Eras and epochs come and go, but some things never change, such as an investor's desire for a positive return. The financial rules applied to investment propositions in the era of J. P. Morgan apply to the era of Bill Gates, Microsoft, and Microsoft .NET technology. At a minimum, an Internet solution that will be undertaken should be subject to ROI analysis, but more intense scrutiny might be warranted. It might be desirable to delve deeper into the financial analysis process and apply the additional analytical methods of net present value (NPV) and internal rate of return (IRR). These two methods, which are covered next, account for the time value of money.

Time Value of Money

One analytical problem with ROI as your sole measure of financial performance is that it doesn't explicitly account for the time value of money. The time value of money theory works like this: a dollar received today is worth more than a dollar received in five years. This is true for three reasons: risk, inflation, and opportunity cost.

Risk

If you have a dollar in hand, you've mitigated the default risk. Following with our example, what if the dollar five years hence failed to materialize? A default would have occurred and your return would be negative. Therefore, a dollar received today has truly been received, something of great value and comfort to the receiver.

Inflation

As a general rule, economies face inflationary, not deflationary pressures. A dollar received today might purchase a cup of coffee, but five years from now, this same dollar in your hand might not be enough to purchase the same cup of coffee.

Opportunity Costs

A dollar received today can be invested, but a dollar received in five years cannot be invested now. This is perhaps the most persuasive argument with respect to the time value of money theory. Opportunity cost is defined as the cost of lost opportunities or the rate of return on the best alternative investment available. Therefore, if you don't have that dollar to invest today, you have missed out on an investment opportunity. Expand this thinking to developing and deploying an Internet solution. If you lack the capital to create an effective Internet solution today, more Internet-savvy competitors might overtake your firm in the marketplace, and you might lose market share for your products. In the worst case, perhaps your firm won't even exist in five years because of its inability to invest in an Internet solution today. A firm that forgoes investing in an Internet solution today does so at its own peril. Customers are finicky and may migrate to a competitor that has undertaken such an investment. To paraphrase thoughts from management consulting guru Tom Peters in a series of popular radio ads, you'll get run over by the competition.

The time value of money is a process in which future cash inflows are penalized by a discount rate that reflects the preceding variables. We need a rate that reduces the value of a future dollar because we're concerned about the risk of receiving the dollar, the effects of inflation, and the opportunity costs. As previously demonstrated, ROI doesn't implicitly apply a discount rate to its calculations. Rather, the ROI calculation is linear and is not linked to when the dollar is actually received. It is of little consequence to the ROI measurement if a dollar is received today, one year from now, or in a decade.

Net Present Value

In the most simplistic terms, an NPV of one dollar or greater suggests that the investment proposition is feasible and should be undertaken. This doesn't suggest that you'll receive only one dollar from all the toil and trouble to develop and deploy an Internet solution. Rather, when a discount rate is applied using NPV, it communicates that you've exceeded the rate of return you set out to achieve for this undertaking. NPV is equal to the present value of future returns penalized by the discount rate minus the present value of the investment. In the example that was summarized in Table 4-1, the Internet solution costs $305,000, the discount rate is 10 percent, the useful life is three years, and the investment returns $150,000 for each of those years. The NPV would be calculated as present value of inflows − cost = NPV. Using the values from Table 4-1, the formula is $373,028 − $305,000 = $68,028.

The bottom line? The NPV for the Internet solution is just over $68,000 when a 10 percent discount rate is used. This would typically be considered an acceptable investment. Finally, NPV is a way to express an investment's return, discounted for the time value of money, in dollar form. Granted, the mathematics used to calculate NPV for an Internet solution is the same as another investment form (such as real estate); only the investment climates are different.

Internal Rate of Return

Believe it or not, IRR is closely related to NPV; they both account for the same financial variables in mathematics. The IRR is the rate of return on an asset investment that accounts for the time value of money. The IRR is the discount rate that equates the present value of future cash flows to the cost of the investment. In general, an IRR that exceeds the firm's marginal cost of capital indicates that the investment should be funded. The firm's marginal cost of capital can be obtained from the accounting department and often reflects the cost of funds to undertake additional borrowing. For example, this might be the interest rate to draw on a commercial line of credit. The IRR calculation is initial investment (T0) = cash flow (T1 – T3) = IRR. Using the values in Table 4-1, the IRR is -$305,000 = $150,000 x 3, which results in 22 percent (a favorable amount). It is this time-adjusted rate of return value that equates the initial investment to the future cash inflows.

Summary

This chapter provided a "pocket" MBA lecture on ROI. Topics addressed herein included defining ROI, exploring different recovery periods, and assessing how costs are allocated to a project. Further explanations focused on defining the time value of money and using more sophisticated financial return measures such as NPV and IRR. What really occurred here, however, was the opportunity to understand core financial valuation techniques in the life of a business decision maker. All business opportunities being considered by a company must make sense, both financially and strategically. With respect to investing in an Internet solution, this chapter provided the tools to assess the financial fit. The book as a whole provides the tools to assess the strategic fit of an Internet investment. The financial foundation provided in this chapter is necessary to proceed to the next chapter, in which the business value of Internet solutions is evaluated. In *Chapter 5, "Creating Business Value,"* you will learn about business value from both a quantitative and qualitative perspective. This includes using Porter's Competitive Forces model and the business value chain model.

Creating Business Value

The desire to create business value from any endeavor is not only what economists call *rational behavior* but clearly is just common sense. The last chapter showed you that all investment propositions (including Internet solutions) must yield a satisfactory return, and this chapter extends that discussion by showing the business value of Internet solutions. In many cases, it's as Tom Peters, renowned management guru and author, proclaims in what he calls "this whacked out world of Internet commerce": keep up or get run over. Keeping up isn't merely about having an Internet solution. It's about having an Internet solution that creates business value. In the context of this chapter, *business value* is discussed as a company's ability to function better—that is, enjoy production efficiencies, shorten the time to market for products, and extend the reach of the company's products—along with other standard measures, such as agility, reliability, and scalability. Additional discussion on management style, employee satisfaction, and customer service improvements is also presented. These discussion points are fodder for business decision makers to make better, more informed decisions.

Internet Solutions Business Issues and Return on Investment

You will recall that return on investment (ROI) was presented in *Chapter 4, "New Rules for Return on Investment,"* from a financial point of view. In that chapter, different investment measures were calculated and you gained the baseline knowledge needed to evaluate the financial impact of different Internet solution investment opportunities. However, there are additional ways to view ROI, because ROI isn't strictly an accounting concept as it was largely presented in *Chapter 4*. It's also a way of thinking qualitatively about improving business processes. As you've seen from earlier chapters, you can't successfully implement an Internet solution until you've examined the core business issues. Take, for example, Gateway Computers. As discussed in *Chapter 2, "Real-World Business Problems Seeking Solutions,"* Gateway had to understand that the Gateway Country stores and the Gateway Web site cross-sell each other. The same could be said for 101communications, with its use of the Web to cross-sell its constituency on new offerings. More important, a business with faulty business fundamentals, such as multiple unfavorable ratios as measured by the DuPont ratio model (the DuPont ratio model is a popular multitiered model of financial ratios such as the Quick and Current Ratios), shouldn't look to an Internet solution as a magic bullet. A poorly managed business in the physical realm will in all likelihood be a poorly managed business in the Internet solution realm.

The qualitative discussion on ROI commences with company performance and continues with production efficiencies, followed by a value-chain discussion in the context of getting products to market (see the section entitled "Speed to Market"). This is followed by a discussion on extending product reach with a focus on Porter's Competitive Forces model.

Better Company Performance

Firms are evolutionary in nature and should always be seeking to improve operations. Although this might sound like a "success" poster hanging in an office, perhaps conveying false enthusiasm, this is an important indicator of a company's ability to successfully leverage its Internet solutions investment to institute a more functional company culture. Firms with a progressive mindset that are committed to deploying Internet solutions are probably enjoying an Internet "dividend." That is, a company culture has likely been created that encourages new thinking and rewards accomplishments. A simple example that many people have witnessed firsthand, electronic communications, serves to make the point. When a company implements an Internet solution, it's highly likely that the employees are strong users of technology. One common example of technology usage is in the form of electronic communications such as e-mail and instant messaging. Electronic communications, more so than paper-based correspondence, have a way of facilitating better communications faster. First, there is the simple act of replying to an e-mail that, when viewed from a time and motion perspective, is much faster than typing and printing a reply memo that is distributed by interoffice mail or courier. The time frame for delivery of an e-mail reply might be seconds. In the case of a paper memo, the time frame for delivery could be hours or days. Clearly, replying by e-mail rather than paper memo is faster and more efficient. Second, organizational theorists believe that electronic communications have created more efficient organizations by breaking down formal chain-of-command structures that allow staff members to communicate with managers and executives. These organizational theorists from the decentralized organization school of thought essentially believe that a business can be more successful when communications flow freely between structural levels. This is due in part to the elimination of communication filters that successive layers of management would otherwise apply to communications that flow through the formal chain of command. In other words, if a line worker has a sentiment he or she wishes to share with an executive, e-mail facilitates this better than formal, paper-based communications. The executive benefits from hearing directly the unfiltered communication from the line worker because the communication from the line worker to the executive hasn't been "spun" for political purposes by a manager who intercepted the communication.

Managers can also manage better because they have better business analysis tools available. These tools can be quantitative tools related to costs and revenues, such as Internet solution reporting. One such tool is Microsoft Commerce Server Business Desk, part of the Microsoft Solution for Internet Business offering. Commerce Server Business Desk is an extensible tool that business managers can use to manage and analyze their Web sites. This tool's features can be used to update pricing information in catalogs and run reports to measure how such changes affect Web site productivity (see *http://www.microsoft.com/commerceserver/evaluation/features/default.asp* for more information). Furthermore, Business Desk allows you to engage in targeted merchandising and promotions (this tool and others are discussed in *Chapter 10, "The Microsoft Solution for Internet Business"*).

These tools can also be of a qualitative nature, allowing the manager to confirm or deny observations based on anecdotal evidence. For example, a manager might observe that ever since the firm implemented an Internet solution, worker productivity has increased because absenteeism has declined. How could that be? Consider that productivity per worker and job satisfaction might have increased with the introduction of this technology. In the case of workers' increasing productivity, consider Gateway, one of the companies profiled in *Chapter 2*. At Gateway, the ordering intranet maps to the same technology used in the Internet solution and has increased workers' productivity.

Perhaps pursuing an Internet solution has allowed unhappy employees to enjoy new job dimensions. For example, an employee with a creative streak and Internet technology aptitude might be a better fit in a new role supporting the Internet solution.

Production Efficiencies

All large firms struggle with managing inventory, especially if a firm is global, with multiple divisions in numerous countries (creating time zone and logistical challenges). Problems can occur with the creation, ordering, storing, and tracking of inventory. However, the same architectural attributes of an Internet solution that allow a customer to place an order for a product can be used to the firm's benefit in gaining production efficiencies. Here's how: Perhaps before the introduction of an Internet solution, the firm had either no inventory management system or one that was outdated. Enter a comprehensive Internet solution under the guise of facilitating electronic commerce with customers. By deconstructing customer order patterns, a business analytics function, the firm can improve its production in the following ways:

- Create products in smaller batches under a "just in time" business model.

- Have producers hold more of the raw materials and partially assembled goods, resulting in lower inventory holding costs to the firm.

- Avoid overproducing goods that are not popular, based on timely customer order pattern feedback.

Speed to Market

An Internet solution can be the basis for linking all the members of a value chain. A value chain depicts the information and material flows needed to get a product to the consumer. Because of the business analytics provided through reporting in an Internet solution, the firm can now make much smarter product decisions. This includes identifying customer preferences earlier and with greater precision. The Internet solution allows the firm to plan more methodically for its markets, again based primarily on business analytics. By effectively avoiding mistakes, such as producing goods that no one will purchase, the firm can stay focused on producing popular goods faster and without distraction.

Extended Product Reach

Features from Michael Porter's popular Competitive Forces model speak directly to using an Internet solution for growing sales of goods: entry barriers, customer bargaining power, and switching costs. Michael Porter, a college professor, wrote the classic book *Competitive Strategy: Techniques for Analyzing Industry and Competitors* (Free Press, 1980), wherein he defined his classic marketing Competitive Forces model. By definition, Porter's Competitive Forces model contains six forces that affect a firm's and an industry's ability to grow, as shown in Figure 5-1.

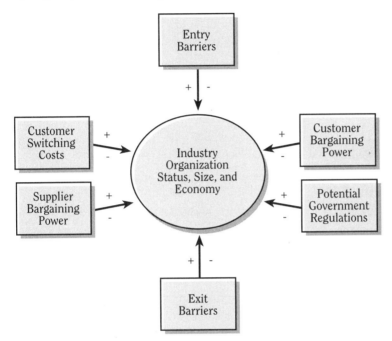

Figure 5-1. *Porter's Competitive Forces model.*

Each force is defined as follows:

- **Entry barriers.** These are obstacles a firm encounters when it attempts to enter an industry or when it is creating or selling a new product or service. Examples of entry barriers include intellectual property patents, copyrights on materials, labor costs, availability of requisite talent, and financial footing. If your firm has the ability and resources to deploy an Internet solution, you can enjoy a competitive advantage over firms with no such capability.

- **Exit barriers.** These are obstacles a firm is likely to encounter when exiting an industry or marketplace. Exit barriers include, but are certainly not limited to, current contractual obligations, customer expectations, and government regulations. That last point was invoked when Gateway Computers attempted to exit European markets and focus its efforts on domestic U.S. operations in the summer of 2001. Gateway learned that it had to maintain its European operations for several months as part of its severance, thus driving up exit costs.

- **Customer bargaining power.** Customer bargaining power is both enhanced and neutralized by the deployment of an Internet solution. The enhancement is that the customer can use aggregate comparison shopping sites that compare pricing from different suppliers, allowing the customer to select the lowest priced product with ease. Conversely, the firm that has deployed an Internet solution that is easy to maintain can dynamically reprice goods, based on these same aggregate comparison shopping sites, and be instantly competitive to the savvy customer.

- **Supplier bargaining power.** Porter refers to this as the force that a firm's suppliers can exert on the organization because of the scarcity of the products and services that the supplier sells, the supplier's price, or the logistics involved in getting the product or service to the firm.

- **Switching costs.** So you're convinced that an Internet solution based on personalization and profiling is suitable for your firm. Here comes the real payoff and added value: saving customer switching costs. The Internet certainly exposes a huge range of purchasing opportunities for the consumer, but an effective Internet solution can actually induce customers to remain loyal to your site. Here's how: When a customer presents basic identification information to a Web site, often in the context of purchasing products using a shopping cart, a profile can be created. Subsequent purchases can be made more easily because the customer's profiled information, stored securely at the firm's Web site, is recalled to autopopulate important transaction fields (address, city, state, ZIP code, telephone number, and credit card information). With respect to personalization, an Internet solution that tracks clicks, purchases, and buyer preferences has the potential to be more appealing to returning customers, building loyalty and implicitly raising switching costs for the customer, thus improving your customer retention. If, for example, a customer has purchased a digital camera from a Web site, on subsequent visits this same customer might be interested in knowing about lower pricing for camera memory cards.

- **Potential government regulations.** In the case of Internet commerce, this might include conduct restrictions (such as privacy policies for customer data) and taxation (such as an Internet sales tax, tariffs, or fees).

Standard Measures

Chapter 4 presented the basics of ROI analysis, which is a standard measure for evaluating investment opportunities and performance. In that same chapter, two other financial measures—internal rate of return (IRR) and net present value (NPV)—also were presented. All three of these measures are financial in nature, but there are other value considerations, including the following:

- **Customer satisfaction.** A qualitative measure that many analysts attempt to quantify using survey and polling methods, customer satisfaction is clearly one of the great assets of an Internet solution. If you believe in the theory that all businesses live and die by referrals in the long run, you will also place great value in customer satisfaction.

- **Business partner satisfaction.** Most business people like to do business with firms similar to their own (culturally speaking, that is). Therefore, progressive companies deploying Internet solutions will have a propensity for seeking out suppliers and vendors that ascribe to the same mindset. The business translation is this: a firm that has a successful Internet solution for its customers will likely find itself attracting and working with like-minded suppliers and vendors, resulting in high levels of satisfaction among business partners.

- **Impressions.** A well-accepted quantitative measure in the world of Internet commerce is the number of customer impressions made. This is casually called the number of eyes looking at the screen or Web site. Both anecdotal and empirical evidence has shown that a large number of customer impressions is favorable because a certain proportion of impressions turn into paying customers.

- **Number of new customers.** Number of customers gained is a quantitative measure that, in one way, reflects the true value of an Internet solution. The relationship is direct with this measure: a large number of new customers attributed to an Internet solution reflects favorably on the value of such a solution.

- **Customer retention.** Closely related to the last point is the number of customers retained. All business people recognize there is a cost to obtaining new customers. This cost declines dramatically when the new customers become repeat customers. By tracking customer retention, you can see exactly how many customers are repeat customers. Retention rates will vary by industry, but this basic measure is a starting point: customers who haven't made a purchase on the Web site in 90 days are considered lost for attrition purposes. One example of an Internet solution with low retention is Internet faxing and voice-mail. Although customers are lured easily by the promise of Internet faxing and voice-mail capabilities, evidence shows that months later these customers are no longer actively using the service.

- **Product availability.** Business decision makers of any stripe recognize there is a real cost, and a high one to say the least, to product stock out. One example of this is book publishing. A publisher would rather flood the market with books than risk having a stock out on the shelves (in this case because the marginal cost to produce greater quantities declines rapidly at high order levels). In the context of a comprehensive Internet solution, the business analytics function can assist business managers in avoiding stock out. More important, this same information can help business managers find the right balance between stock out and carrying too much inventory.

- **Promotion costs.** This cost category can bedevil the financial results of an Internet solution. Many smart minds, including graduates from the best MBA programs, have struggled with holding the line on promotional costs. However, all agree that some marketing expenses in the form of promotion must be incurred to drive customer traffic to a Web site. Traditional promotional avenues such as public advertising (display, billboard, radio, and TV) and trade show participation have been met with varying degrees of success, and often disappointment. However, experience has shown that having Web page links from a category leader back to your Web site is especially effective. For example, a leading computer software vendor might provide links to its consulting partners. This example is a key component of a successful Internet solution wherein the software provider shares its short list of preferred solution providers in implementing an Internet solution (see *Chapter 10*). This is the cornerstone of the Microsoft Solution for Internet Business offering: referring trusted consulting partners to customers seeking to successfully implement an Internet solution.

- **Gross margins and net profit margins.** In this era of pro forma financial reporting where the clear distinction is drawn between gross margins (revenues before many general, administrative, and marketing costs as well as interest and taxes) and net profit (the bottom line on the income statement), profits are still important. This is obvious, but there is currently a flight to fund only Internet investment propositions that are presently profitable, not those that promise profitability at a future date.

- **Distribution costs.** The delivery side of an Internet solution invokes production mechanisms that allow the business to distribute goods more efficiently. For example, an Internet bookseller might never stock the actual book but rather have it shipped directly from the publisher to the consumer. This reduces inventory costs as a working capital component and even real estate costs (due to not having to maintain large warehouses).

Value Chain

Another look at creating business value is provided by *value chain analysis*. Considering the activities that a firm performs to produce and sell a product, it's an impressive set of tasks. There must be successful outcomes at the design, production, marketing, fulfillment, and customer support stages (and your list might even include more task areas). As displayed in Figure 5-2, each of these areas adds value to the product you provide to customers; hence, the value-added nature of the value chain.

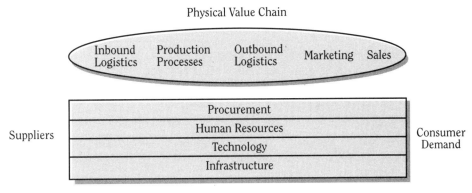

Figure 5-2.   *Value chain details.*

Across the top of the figure, the value chain elements are displayed left to right from supplier to consumer. From top to bottom, the infrastructure components, including technology, are depicted. A supplier supplies raw or partially finished goods. The firm coordinates the inbound flow of these materials. A production process occurs at the firm and the outbound logistics process occurs (coordinating distribution and so on). The downstream functions of marketing and sales follow. The top-to-bottom view speaks to traditional functional business activities such as procurement, human resources management, technology development, and firm infrastructure.

Although value chain is well understood in the physical product realm, where raw materials are manufactured into final goods, the virtual world of information isn't as straightforward. David Kosiur, in his 1997 book *Understanding Electronic Commerce* (Microsoft Press), created the *virtual value chain,* as shown in Figure 5-3.

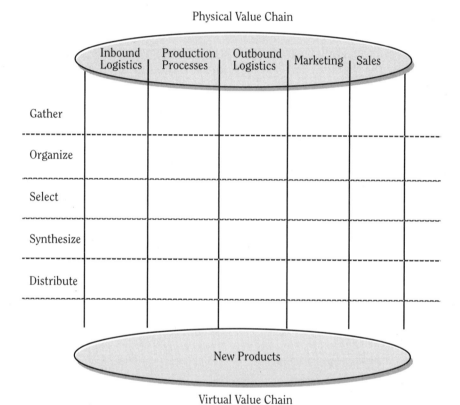

Figure 5-3.   *Kosiur's virtual value chain.*

Five additional functions are added to the virtual value chain to create value: gathering, organizing, selecting, synthesizing, and distributing. Kosiur further believes that the virtual value chain can be viewed as a matrix, with each cell (the intersection between columns and rows in Figure 5-3) representing an opportunity to add value.

If the product that you sell is information, as it is for VersusLaw in *Chapter 2,* your challenge is to add value to this information before distribution to the consumer. In the case of VersusLaw, this is accomplished in at least two ways: gathering and enhancing.

Value Added: Content Aggregation

Content aggregation is a value-added function provided by a firm that has deployed an Internet solution. This section provides two examples of this: VersusLaw and the U.S. Internal Revenue Service (IRS).

By gathering information from numerous legal sources including courts (local, district, county, state, and federal) and other legal service providers, VersusLaw creates value by saving customers time. Attorneys seeking legal research can look to VersusLaw to be a single source of legal information so that they don't have to perform this gathering function.

Another example related to information gathering is the IRS, as covered in *Chapter 2*. Much of the IRS mission involves the dissemination of information. Volumes and volumes of tax code and guidance are posted at the IRS Web site (*www.irs.gov*). Practically speaking, there are few larger online libraries than that of the IRS.

Value Added: Synthesis

The ability to traverse aggregated information and allow the customer to find the relevant information quickly is a value-added process known as *synthesis*. A significant value-added feature from VersusLaw is the way in which it synthesizes, analyzes, and summarizes research. This analytical function makes the raw legal research much more valuable to the researching attorney by saving time and "cutting to the chase" of the legal matter. The attorney is certainly not obligated to accept VersusLaw's opinion rendering, but it's a starting point from which to work more efficiently.

Summary

This chapter focused on several forms of creating business value in the context of Internet solutions. Much of the business value discussion was qualitative, such as company performance improving as a result of better management approaches. Production and speed to market were discussed. Extending product reach was discussed in the context of Porter's Competitive Forces model, and several components of the model were related directly to Internet solutions. Standard valuation measures, including some financial measures, were discussed next. The chapter concluded with a discussion on the product and virtual value chain and how that relates to Internet solutions and the creation of business value. In the next chapter, you'll look at a host of technical topics related to creating an Internet solution. Specific emphasis is placed on making the Internet solution dynamic.

The Microsoft Solution Set

Businesses are no longer judged solely by their ability to generate revenue; instead, the ability to secure and retain customers is becoming the primary success criteria for businesses everywhere. With the expansion of the Internet into every facet of customer commerce, it is becoming imperative to use the Internet as a powerful way to provide the best customer experience possible. What used to be the province of service boutiques or luxury goods sellers is now achievable by mom-and-pop stores. As customers seek differentiation among all those who vie for their business, the ability to deliver the best possible customer experience pays off with better figures on the bottom line.

In this section we explain how a basic Web presence can be expanded into a dynamic, personalized extension of your business, and how industry-leading technology delivers an enhanced customer experience and improves your ability to connect with customers. You will also see how online retail shopping can become a pleasure for both customers and sales staff, bringing together the best of all worlds into a comprehensive business-to-customer (B2C) sales and delivery powerhouse. Finally, the use of Microsoft's technology as the bedrock of your Internet presence is explained, showing you how the pieces come together as an integrated whole.

Benefits Analysis: Creating a Base Dynamic Internet Presence

Most companies look to improve their bottom line by either increasing revenues or cutting costs. Traditional business theory suggested these were mutually exclusive options, because increasing revenue usually meant spending more money on advertising, researching and developing new products, or merger and acquisition activities to expand a product family or business line. Cutting costs was incompatible with increased advertising or product-related expenditures and was often portrayed to investors and employees as "doing more with less" or "working smarter."

The Internet has profoundly changed the ways that companies can do business with customers by supporting both strategies: Companies can pursue new customers, new markets, and new products using less money than before (both for capital expenditures and marginal costs). They can also reduce costs by automating many traditional business operations. By enabling Internet-based business, companies are finding it easier to reap the benefits for themselves and their customers. Companies that are reluctant to adopt the new business solutions will find it harder to compete effectively for customer attention and customer dollars, or to develop a competitive advantage using product or service differentiation. Finally, these benefits extend outward to customers and trading partners and inward to company employees, providing improved efficiencies and business processes that directly impact profitability.

In this chapter you will see how strong content management, centralized security, and robust development tools and rapid deployment models provide the components you need to improve customer relationships and thereby improve your own business model. This foundation also provides the underpinnings for building a strong retail model, which pulls all these requirements together and adds its own specialized challenges to be successful.

Content Management: Customer, Partner, and Business Benefits

Content management enables companies to quickly and efficiently build, deploy, and maintain highly dynamic Internet, intranet, and extranet Web sites. Content management benefits extend outward to customers and trading partners and inward to IT and Web server staff. The overwhelming complexity of Web sites makes effective Web communication extremely expensive to achieve using manual processes. To realize the benefits of Web communication, businesses need tools that increase the manageability and reduce the cost of publishing content.

Web content management (WCM) systems accomplish this by providing tools that automate the publishing process and providing business users with the ability to create content when they recognize a customer need for information. The business case for a content management solution starts with the cost savings generated by improved Web development and publishing processes. A WCM system helps companies do the following:

- Reduce content update costs and improve the frequency of information publication.

- Increase Web content quality with workflow and approval processes.

- Standardize content structures and maintain design control and branding across an organization.

- Maximize effectiveness of team skills by enabling business users to publish their own content and enabling technical staff to work on site infrastructure.

- Leverage existing enterprise technologies and skills to deploy Web applications.

- Reduce site creation, maintenance, and enterprise rollout costs by creating automated processes.

With a robust content management system, you can do the following:

- Empower content providers within an organization to create, manage, and publish their own content, and enable IT departments to quickly deploy scalable dynamic sites.

- Deliver dynamic content for multiple audiences, devices, and purposes across enterprise Web sites.

- Personalize content to ensure a positive user experience for prospects, customers, employees, and business partners.

- Deploy rapidly, and provide greater reliability and reduced maintenance costs.

- Consolidate multiple departmental intranet sites into a single, unique site.

- Manage an increasing content load for the popular Internet site without adding developers.

These benefits are perhaps the most highly visible improvements that can be made to your existing business processes, and those that can provide the quickest return on investment (ROI) by reducing internal costs associated with Internet-based business.

Developing Online Collaboration and Community

Everyone works with documents, but not everyone has the ability to use technology to structure how he or she works with colleagues on these documents. The process from document creation through intranet publishing can be a string of disjointed actions, unconnected with business processes. Enter the world of online collaboration and online community. An effective business system includes collaboration and community tools that are used to create and manage documents and allows users to create customized "personal" workspaces to organize and present information that is especially relevant to them, such as project- or workgroup-specific information.

Some of the key features and benefits of such systems are as follows:

- People can quickly browse through information by categories, rather than document by document.

- Users can subscribe to new or changing information in fields of interest, such as particular product lines, news or press releases, or technical bulletins.

- Anyone along a document creation and publication chain can check documents in and out or be restricted from seeing sensitive documents prior to publication.

- The system tracks a document's version history, and users or administrators can view earlier versions or view the history as an abstract.

- An electronic document approval process can be put in place for documents prior to publication to ensure consistency or standards review.

- Finally, the system must publish documents or make them available to subscribers both within the company on your intranet and to customers, business partners, or surfers who contact you through your Web site on the Internet.

The goal of these features is to create an online environment where content contributors can have quick and easy access to materials and publish them without relying on "normal channels." For example, a Web article about a new product might need to be worked on by several people: the person creating the text, a graphics designer for any pictures or illustrations, a product manager or product marketing manager, a Web page designer, and finally an IT Webmaster. These five people will need a central place where they can access the Web page and make changes rapidly, based on feedback from each other. An online collaboration system allows them to do this without relying on hard-copy printouts being routed through interoffice mail or sending electronic copies through an ever-lengthening chain of e-mail addresses.

Providing Solid Search Capabilities

Locating information in any organization can be challenging. In addition, wading through the different forms, file formats, and storage locations that information requires (documents on file servers, Hypertext Markup Language [HTML] pages on Web servers, or e-mail on messaging servers) and finding what you need when you need it can be difficult. People must have a consistent place to access needed information—in a structured way that makes sense. In addition, the information should be in a central location where such information is aggregated, organized, and searchable. This is true whether it is your customers looking for engine maintenance manuals or your employees looking for the holiday schedule in your human resources manual. An organization's information is usually stored in multiple locations in a variety of formats. Even if a server infrastructure allows searches across multiple data stores, often only limited text searches are available. It can also be difficult to determine whether the results that these simple searches provide are relevant.

A robust search engine allows you to index an intranet site and access key content from a broader set of enterprise information. In addition to having one comprehensive place in the portal to search, you can also set the portal to have information come to you using information subscription—directly delivering new and changed content notifications. The system should allow users to select among the Subscriptions, Category Browsing, and Best Bets options in search results, and the system itself should be extensible using third-party products for specialized search and notification needs. These features include the following:

- A single location to search for information stored in many different places.
- Keyword searches that search the full text of a document and the document's properties.
- Browsing by topic (categories) to find information.
- Automatic categorization of documents.
- Best Bet classification for documents that are highly relevant to a search.
- Subscriptions to keep users updated on useful information.

Whether you are searching for something specific or just browsing through a group of related documents, your search engine should make finding information easier with several features that make searches faster and more successful.

Creating a Personal Internet Experience

Customers want information. The majority of Internet users go online to find information—information to get their job done or to help make purchase decisions. They want information personalized to their needs and interests. E-commerce sites that do not recognize these user requirements will fail. One key method of personalization is providing content that is personalized for groups and individual users. For example, customers interested in servers see articles about server performance and benchmarking. This type of information improves the user experience, encourages repeat visits, and helps speed purchase decisions. The answer comes in the form of personalization tools.

Personalization tools provide a more relevant user experience. With personalization tools in an Internet-based system, site visitors can choose content preferences and automatically see links related to areas of interest. To maintain a high level of personalization, e-commerce sites must be dynamic. Personalized sites cannot be served well from a flat-file system. Instead, sites must be assembled from a dynamic database as users request pages. Without this dynamic functionality, the cost of maintaining a highly personalized, content-rich site is prohibitive.

Personalization tools also allow businesses to deploy information faster. In addition to empowering consumers by providing robust information and a personalized browsing experience, sites must also empower business users. Businesses must be able to quickly and cost-effectively deploy highly dynamic and personalized e-business Web sites. Business users must be able to publish their own content—including rich product catalog pages, news, and articles—using familiar tools. This empowers a business to communicate directly with prospects, customers, partners, and co-workers, by publishing rich, targeted content directly to a variety of Internet, intranet, and extranet applications.

Building a Robust Internet Presence

Once you start building your Internet business system, you should be sure it can handle increased workloads as your business grows. Your Internet solution should provide a well-integrated package containing the application development environment, Web services, security, and scalability you need to grow your presence as customer demand increases. You should be able to build new and versatile solutions using the most complete set of Internet technologies available. It should also be engineered specifically to let companies reliably and economically use emerging technologies as they arise.

A properly designed Internet system infrastructure should enable the creation of a flexible system for urgent business requirements. The system should reduce the level of duplication and streamline the interfaces between the company and its suppliers, customers, and partners. The system should also increase your system's availability using high-availability technologies such as clustering, which let you link servers to support specific tasks.

These all combine to create a robust system that can scale to meet higher demands for service and new applications, or provide high availability to customers and partners who need real-time or near–real-time access to applications and information.

Customer Relationship Management

Business communication is moving so quickly that the traditional lines of responsibility are blurring. More and more employees are making decisions and communicating directly with customers, prospects, and partners. Internet, intranet, and extranet sites can no longer afford to be static information suppliers. Web sites must be dynamic business applications that enable effective peer-to-peer, business-to-business (B2B), and business-to-consumer (B2C) communications. Technology can make building Web applications fast, but only people empowered to create and manage their own content can make Web applications work.

Integration between customer relationship management (CRM) and WCM systems dramatically improves business communications with customers, prospects, and partners. An integrated solution provides organizations with a personalized Web site experience that combines rich, targeted, dynamically assembled content with customer information from a CRM database. Businesses that combine CRM and WCM systems are able to build Web applications that quickly and efficiently address the needs of customers with rich, targeted content. The CRM system manages customer data, customer relationships, and customer contact initiatives and enables business users to act on that data, whereas the WCM system handles the authoring, delivery, and management of relevant and timely content.

Through an integrated Web application that takes advantage of the unique features of CRM and WCM, businesses can do the following:

- Improve customer service by better understanding customer information requirements.

- Better communicate product knowledge to customers through distributed publishing.

- Deliver a complete business communication application to business users, prospects, customers, and partners.

- Empower business users to access, update, and monitor diverse information about customers, from simple contact information to purchasing preferences.

- Enable sales and customer support to quickly respond to requests and anticipate the needs of prospects and customers.

With integrated solutions, communication of customer information occurs over targeted Web sites built and managed by the content management system, whether communicating technical product information in a customer care application or detailed sales tools to partners over a specially designed extranet.

Sites with relevant content attract visitors, quickly get visitors the information they need, and keep them coming back regularly. By providing content-rich, well-managed Web sites, businesses deliver greater value to customers, prospects, and partners.

Collecting Business Analytics on Key Performance Indicators

The key benefits for business analytics are twofold: to respond quickly to change, and to enable smarter business decisions that lead to a competitive advantage. Business managers require both sophisticated decision support and the ability to take action in real time to provide customers and partners with a superior Web experience. Ideally your business system records each interaction between your site and your customers and feeds into your business analytics system, thereby providing insight to business managers and enabling them to make timely and effective business decisions. You can also develop, deploy, and monitor customized marketing campaigns or strategies to improve your ability to reach existing or potential customers with products or services. This helps you reduce costs by spending money wisely on campaigns that produce an improved ROI, and it helps your company be more effective by delivering messages to customers who will actually benefit from the product or service.

Your system should include a robust data warehousing system that incorporates all site data, including click-stream usage (which customers click on which products, and of those, which result in purchases) and purchase history—in addition to campaign, user profile, product, legacy, and external data—into a centralized repository for sophisticated, real-time, and report-driven analyses. Your business analysis tools should include built-in analysis tools for reporting on critical business metrics, with drill-down reporting available through integration with other business system components. Your solution should also provide site managers with insight into site effectiveness and the data needed to manage merchandising, personalization, and user customization aspects of the site.

You should be able to mine collected data to identify hidden trends and new customer segments so that you have a thorough understanding of these customers and their business. This allows you to determine lucrative cross-sell or up-sell opportunities and dynamically recommend these to customers as they navigate your site. This further helps create personalized sites that make customers feel unique, giving the positive impression that you understand their interests and can help suggest things to them that will prove useful, valuable, or informative. Business managers can gain additional insight into user behavior by viewing identified segments, understanding the most critical user properties for the segment.

Reducing Development and Management Costs

Sites must be fast to deploy and fast to change. They must be built with tools familiar to your team and must properly use people's skill sets. Business managers must be in control of site content and customer profiling, and they must be able to make changes to content, special offers, and user profiles based on user feedback and site analysis. Web developers and designers must be in control of site usability, architecture, and design. All these factors can quickly balloon your project's costs far beyond your budget.

Your solution must provide lower development and management costs, otherwise you will fight a losing battle as your Web site grows and the document management tasks mount. There are several areas that will provide reduced development and management costs over time.

Support for Rapid Application Development Systems

Most businesses developing new systems are looking for rapid application development (RAD) support. RAD is the concept that products can be developed faster and of higher quality by doing the following:

- Gathering user requirements and prototyping designs early and often, using focus groups of users for feedback.

- Designing reusable software components, such as navigation bars.

- Less formality in reviews and other team communication.

- Using tools that encourage modular design and reuse of components.

RAD support can be found in sample templates or solution sites, requirement-gathering tools, prototyping tools, computer-aided software engineering tools, integrated development environments, groupware for communication among development members, and testing tools. RAD usually embraces object-oriented methodology, which inherently encourages software reuse. The most popular object-oriented programming languages are offered in visual programming packages often described as providing RAD.

These systems enable rapid development and reuse of software components, making it cheaper to design and develop projects without a lot of custom code, which can be expensive to design and maintain.

Creating Interoperable Systems for Existing Applications and Data

Most businesses already have existing systems and applications, many of which include proprietary access methods. Extending those applications to build new e-business initiatives is not an easy task (and is often not authorized). Thus it is imperative that any system you invest in is able to interoperate with these systems. This is considered different from integration, in which the systems contain common code or become part of a single code base; instead, interoperability allows each system or application to be independent of other systems, but a series of intermediaries or application "glue" is used to connect systems together. The system you choose must be capable of building this glue or being part of a linking application.

The benefit is then extended to the legacy data and applications you already have in your company. You can leverage these applications and their data to develop powerful new applications that enable your customers, partners, and employees to work together synergistically.

Creating a Single Solution for Both Transacted and Nontransacted Corporate Sites

An Internet solution must be able to interact both with systems that support transaction coordinators and those that do not. In this context, a *transaction* is an interaction between systems that uses specific mechanisms to ensure that the correct conditions for the exchange exist. It has a finite beginning and ending, otherwise the transaction as a whole is rolled back. For example, when money is moved between two accounts at a bank, the transaction consists of debiting one account and crediting another. If for some reason the transaction cannot take place, such as insufficient funds in the debited account or system unavailability on the credited account, the entire transaction is rolled back and no money is transferred. This ensures integrity for the business system as well as accountability to the bank's customers.

This level of integrity is costly but necessary for some businesses, such as banks, insurance companies, or supply chain mechanisms. Smaller businesses that do not carry large inventories or do not need absolute transactional integrity do not have these systems in place. Anyone who wants to conduct business across the Internet should invest in a system that supports both transacted and nontransacted models, depending on the business partner's model.

Extending Internet Presence to a Variety of Devices

Web-enabling applications for customers, partners, and employees is a great start to enabling e-business. However, as the rate of change seems to be increasing exponentially every year, there is already a need to make your applications and data available to other devices and other browsers—in other words, to any device, anywhere, at any time.

An Internet-ready solution should be able to extend its presence to a variety of devices and extend its applications, enterprise data, and intranet content into the realm of the mobile user. It brings the power of the corporate intranet to the latest generation of mobile devices, so users can securely access their e-mail, contacts, calendar, tasks, or any intranet line-of-business application in real time, wherever they happen to be. It allows developers to use the existing investment in the corporate intranet or an online computing solution by easily building connectors and services for any data server type or application.

Developers can use existing skills and tools to create new wireless applications and content based on a highly extensible architecture. Most important, an Internet server with wireless extensions provides users with the ability to make the device that they already own immediately more useful. It offers broad support for multiple mobile devices as well as flexibility for new generations of devices such as smart tablets, voice recognition systems, and embedded systems.

Ability to Create and Consume XML Web Services

Extensible Markup Language (XML) is an emerging technology that is rapidly changing the face of business. XML looks like HTML but is not tied to presentation in a browser; instead, it is a data description language that can be read and understood by people or by another program, and can be shaped and crafted in any manner that proves useful. This flexibility makes it an ideal neutral language for exchanging data between different systems within a business or between businesses.

XML Web services are revolutionizing how applications talk to other applications—or more broadly, how computers talk to other computers—by providing a universal data format that lets data be easily adapted or transformed. XML-based standards, which include Simple Object Access Protocol (SOAP) and Universal Description, Discovery, and Identification (UDDI), comprise the open methodology for application-to-application communication known as XML Web services. With XML Web services, not only can applications share data, they can also invoke capabilities from other applications without regard for how other applications were built. Sharing data through XML allows them to be independent of each other while giving them the ability to loosely link themselves into a collaborative group that performs a particular task.

Web sites are about presenting information to a user: they are communication vehicles for servers to talk to users. XML Web services, on the other hand, offer a direct means for applications to interact with other applications. Applications hosted internally as well as on remote systems can communicate using the Internet without requiring human intervention or direction. This saves time, improves internal processes, and enables real-time access to a user's information.

Providing Enterprise-Level Services and Support

When you invest in an Internet solution partnership, you should ensure that you work with technology providers and system integration partners to help you plan, develop, and deploy your system. These partners should provide help through every stage of the technology planning, deployment, and support process. Ideally, they will specialize in providing real-life IT solutions: e-commerce, enterprise application planning, distributed network architecture computing, and more. Your support partners should have the experience and expertise to align your IT vision and business goals. The following sections detail some of the services you should look for.

Assessment and Review Services

If your organization is in the early planning stages for a major operational system, Assessment and Review Services provide in-depth evaluation of business requirements, plans, architectures, and designs of operational systems and environments. This early-stage service allows you to identify and mitigate risks and realize benefits quickly.

Planning, Architecture, and Design Services

Do you need help building a solution from the ground up? These services will help you create plans for business solutions and technical architecture as well as design infrastructure and mission-critical applications. Based on a proven approach, this service includes assessment and review documents that are developed in-house and extend beyond the scope of Assessment and Review Services.

Proof-of-Concept Services

After you have finished the planning and design stage of a solution, Proof-of-Concept Services will deliver a prototype or pilot for a particular project. This service empowers you to mitigate technical risks and accelerate the formation of a project team prior to the development or deployment of your IT solution.

Implementation Services

Your partnership should include agreement on how much design, coding, and testing will be allocated to each member of the partnership. No matter who you partner with, you need assurances that the solutions partners are experienced in designing this type of system, that their coders are knowledgeable and experienced with this type of business system and the tools and software needed to develop it, and that the partners can test the code, not just on a PC in a lab somewhere but on site or in a simulation environment that takes into account all the variables in your system.

This should not be an "extra," or something that is thrown into the discussion at the last minute; instead it should be discussed when the project groundwork is laid, and you should receive assurances that the partner you are working with has top-of-the-line credentials. This is your business, after all.

Deployment Services

Your partners should not just be "code jockeys," but should also have experience with enterprise-level systems and the supporting infrastructure. They need to know how your systems interoperate and how to work within any system constraints. This knowledge contributes directly to planning for solution deployment; your solution partner must understand how to plan for system capacity (and its attendant scaling and availability concerns), system and data security, network firewalls and topology issues, and hardware and software infrastructure.

These factors all go beyond focusing just on what needs to be built and go toward understanding how to build it and how to minimize complexity or fragility. It would not do to have the best content management system in the world if it can handle only 100 subscribers or is regularly unavailable because of system downtime or network bandwidth issues. Make sure your partner has this knowledge and familiarity with the entire network, not just the server.

Operations Services

When you partner with solution providers, they should be able to help you with operational services for your solution that include training and guidance on how the system is maintained on a daily basis as well as long-term monitoring. You should discuss target goals for system availability or uptime, baseline performance goals, page views or transactions per minute, or other metrics that can be built into the system or monitored by existing services.

Operations planning must also include the more mundane but equally important tasks of backup and disaster recovery, ongoing system maintenance with software upgrades or solution enhancements, and system expansion recommendations for increasing capacity by scaling up, scaling out, or increasing system availability through redundancy and elimination of single-point-of-failure weaknesses. This type of system planning is done for the long term, not the short term, and will be of continued benefit long after the solution is up and running.

Support Planning

Sometimes a solution partner will tell you that once a system is installed and running, you're on your own—the reasons cited usually include the idea that too many things can happen, the systems are no longer under the sole control of the provider, and so forth. However, reputable solution providers don't send you a "thanks for the memories" card at the end of the project; they are able to provide you with support and planning for the life span of the solution.

Support planning services start at the postdeployment phase and cover the system's overall health and operational status. This includes providing guaranteed response times on trouble calls or system alerts, problem isolation, troubleshooting and preemptive maintenance, and even ongoing system and software updates, service packs, and patch installations. These services complement your existing IT service and support staff with people knowledgeable about the new business solution, and they provide the added benefit of knowledge transfer from the services staff to your own department. The most powerful weapon you can have is the ability to bring in the experts quickly. When a system hiccup means money lost, you don't want to spend time on hold waiting for the next available front-line technician.

Custom Solution Services

Other needs can be met with custom solution services for your business, such as short-term technical project planning or postdeployment service-level agreements or guaranteed response times.

Summary

Building and deploying a Web-based e-business solution results in many benefits: lower costs, faster deployments, better content control, and information personalization as well as integration with existing data and systems for maximum ROI. The sum of these efforts brings a greater level of satisfaction with your business from all groups that you interact with, including customers, partners, and employees, and ensures that you will continue to be successful in your primary goal: conducting business and making money. In the next chapter, we'll examine how a retail Web presence has a different set of considerations to meet, from product cataloging to product delivery systems, and how specific tools and services help tie together disparate business systems into a coordinated whole.

Benefits Analysis: Retail

The pace of change in today's business world is faster than ever. New business models, new competitors, mergers and acquisitions, and new partnerships are compelling chief executive officers (CEOs) to make decisions quickly and chief technology officers (CTOs) to implement new business solutions quickly. Additional demands on organizations include outsourcing and virtual organizations as well as promotion and service needs. To succeed in this fluid environment, retailers must have the agility to adapt their business strategy rapidly in response to changing market conditions.

The primary goal for retailers moving to an online Internet presence is to create systems that address business challenges in the industry today and can evolve quickly to meet the demands of the marketplace. Typically, businesses moving to Internet systems want customers to be able to obtain the same level of service over the Internet that they would receive had they contacted the business through any other sales channel. Thus the key goals in building retail Internet systems are to create solutions that increase customer satisfaction, remove barriers to new customer acquisition, streamline order management, and reduce long-term IT costs.

In this chapter you'll see how an online retail presence extends your ability to do business and achieve economies in business, by both providing your customers with better products and services and reducing the overall cost of doing business. You will also see how specific retail solutions can best meet your needs when you decide to implement specific solutions in *Chapter 8, "Microsoft Frameworks."*

Catalog Management

Most retail businesses have difficulty maintaining the integration of inventory systems, catalog sales, and storefront operations as a unified whole. Instead, there are entire departments or divisions of people who work in an isolated fashion, maintaining separate business systems with redundant sets of data. The chores of coordinating product lines, stock keeping units (SKUs), and inventory at retail stores and warehouses are huge tasks. Further, it is difficult, if not impossible, to provide customized catalogs for retail customers, vendors, and trading partners that accurately reflect the choices available to them and are based on customer preferences. Even with call centers and dedicated account managers, it is nearly impossible to maintain real-time information about products, pricing, and availability, not to mention order status or product-tracking capabilities.

Enter the world of online retail catalog management. Catalogs are used for product and merchandise data, encompassing both externally focused information for retail consumers and internally focused information for suppliers, trading partners, and company personnel. When these systems are automated and integrated, powerful new opportunities arise to present information to customers in ways that cannot be matched by traditional brick-and-mortar outlets, including analyzing customer behaviors and effectiveness of marketing programs. The combination of e-commerce and bricks-and-mortar retail ensures that products and product information are readily available to consumers and that users can browse and purchase products that are not in stock in shops, allowing retail businesses to gain additional sales. It also enables the ability to push products with higher margins or time-sensitive products that might otherwise go unpurchased.

In essence, retail businesses are looking to build a solution that will enable the company to meet a strategic goal—reaching out to customers through the Internet and extending the retail experience into the user's home or office. To do this, they need the ability to better communicate with customers to learn their preferences and the flexibility to use this knowledge to deliver a better customer experience. The main benefit is being able to build a more personal relationship with customers—to determine what they want and then personalize the retail experience to meet those needs. Once the preferences are understood on an individual level, a business can use this knowledge to drive improvements to the customer experience across the company, whether using the Internet or using a retail store. This could be accomplished by customizing product selection or by targeting specific promotions to frequent customers. Either method improves the ability of a business to react and respond better to customer needs, thus encouraging ongoing customer loyalty.

Product catalogs are the primary means for users to find and view product information within the business-to-business (B2B) portal; therefore synchronization between these catalogs and manufacturing systems is essential. Offering personalized catalogs ensures that shoppers see the appropriate products and pricing structure, depending on their classification. For example, high-volume customers would be presented with pricing discounts that wouldn't be available to lower volume purchasers, or sports apparel customers could be presented with information on adventure-oriented tour packages. A custom catalog is then created for each customer, including only those products created from a single master catalog. Another tactic is to build up-sell opportunities based on user preferences and purchase history. A particular customer might be more likely to purchase options or add-on packages when shown the additional value they add to a product, or he or she might bump up to a higher class product in order to maintain a particular image. Both tactics are useful in presenting additional sales opportunities and additional revenue on the same customer visit.

All of this can be done by combining catalog management with user personalization, allowing businesses to deliver the content that is most relevant to a particular customer. Integration of content management with catalog management makes it easier to keep catalogs and other information current, a task that has often been difficult to manage and achieve, especially with catalog content running into the hundreds of pages.

One of the next steps in creating a personalized experience is to sift through data generated by the customer's interaction with the Internet presence and create specific profiles or general customer trends based on that data. To do this, you need a set of robust data mining tools.

Data Mining Tools

With most traditional marketing methods, it has been difficult to determine the rate of return based on advertising dollars spent. Although a response ratio of 1 to 2 percent is considered average, and 4 to 5 percent is considered outstanding, there was little to indicate just what motivating event led to a sale: was it the direct mail piece, the radio advertisement, or the newspaper flyer?

Retail Internet technology has changed all that. With the appropriate technology and data mining tools, it is now possible to obtain real-time metrics on customer trends and purchasing patterns based on activities at a Web site. Most traditional Web sites lack adequate integration with both ends of the retail Internet presence: the Web site and its content, and the back-end inventory and transaction systems. Where previous sites provided few tracking or usage statistics, data mining functions enable businesses to collect data on users' shopping and browsing habits. This data can be used to target the products and advertisements featured on the site's home page to individual users, and it provides real-world metrics on marketing campaign effectiveness.

For example, new technology innovations include data mining functions and associated interpretation and reporting techniques that enable marketers to track habits and trends for both registered and anonymous users. Using the reporting and analysis functions on a retail Web site, marketing team members can make intelligent decisions on ads or promotions and reconfigure the site to drive traffic to target areas, or they can move content to high-traffic areas. This feedback loop facilitates managing the selection and delivery of specific site content such as advertisements, discounts, related sells, or direct mail to users according to a set of business rules. It also makes the best use of time and other limited resources and enables the efficient use of marketing dollars in well-targeted campaigns. The analytics then integrate tightly to select specific users to be targeted with specific content such as custom catalogs or special offers on cross-sell or up-sell campaigns.

Marketing executives can also benefit from improved reporting and data analysis capabilities, and they now have the ability to react to this information and close the loop in real time through the site management capabilities. To be effective, you need raw data reports on measures such as time spent on any one page or total time on the site, as well as analyzed data reports such as prediction models for future customer behavior and segment models for past customer behavior. Executives can empower line-of-business managers to determine what is working and what isn't in a particular product or campaign, and to go further and determine why they are getting those results. They can likewise determine why they might not be achieving their quarterly or long-term business or sales goals. The retail Web data that is available goes much deeper than just traffic volume. In a sophisticated e-commerce solution, reporting requirements should include tracking responses to promotions and e-mail campaigns, not only by capturing click-stream analysis for each link in the e-mail, but by taking it one step further and identifying the percentage of click-throughs for each link that resulted in purchases.

The solution should also monitor the number of active, inactive, and new users and have the ability to examine several other characteristics of user behavior, such as visit length and most popular pages—for both purchasers and nonpurchasers. This can then be tied back to purchase and sale data to track sales of featured items based on where each item is located on the site. Managers can also see the browse-to-buy ratio for a product, view the top-selling and least-selling items by geographical area, and even get reports on the number of times a person visits the site before making a purchase.

If site visitors aren't inspired to purchase items in one area of your site but have increased purchase activity in another area of your site, you can work to bring users to that area earlier in their site exploration. It all comes back to the same theme—learning what your customers want and using this knowledge in real time to meet these needs in a manner that benefits both you and the consumers. This makes your Web site more efficient and directly contributes to meeting your corporate goals, whether they are increased revenue, lower cost of business, or improvement of the bottom line. The customers also benefit by finding goods and services more quickly, finding exactly the items they are looking for, and enjoying a good customer experience that leads to return visits and additional purchases. A retail Web site should integrate its data mining capabilities not just to generate reports and metrics, but also to provide actions based on that information—in this case, providing the ability to market new products or opportunities to customers. The purpose of all the data mining, interpolation, and reporting capabilities is to better understand the motivations and behaviors of your customers. As you begin to better understand them, you can close the loop by making improvements to the site. If you see that certain content is very popular, you can easily create a new promotion tied to the content, knowing that you have the tools to monitor response and make incremental changes to the promotion, or to further refine the campaign by running slightly different promotions based on other aspects of user behavior.

This then enables you to innovate and test your assumptions and at the same time minimize the potential for any negative risks. You can monitor results in almost real time, and enable your business managers to make rapid corrections or refinements until you're satisfied with the results. The level of integration in a sophisticated retail Web site enables you to close the loop extremely quickly, which minimizes any potential long-term negative impact.

Customer Targeting Tools

Not only can a retail Internet presence provide new products and opportunities to customers based on their contacts with your company, but it can also create new opportunities for your own sales and marketing force. This gives them back what is all too often in short supply: the time to sell products and services, rather than trying to extract useful reports and sales strategies from different back-end business systems. You can do this by using targeting tools, which take the data and reports generated by data mining tools and create specific sets of actions based on those results. The data from these tools can be used by itself, or it can be integrated with a third-party customer relationship management (CRM) solution. CRM is used to fill the gap between customer data and total customer experience and is one of the premiere ways of tying together various customer contact organizations to present a single and consistent customer experience with a business. Some examples include the following:

- **Create account executive profiles.** You can set up profiles so that a specific representative sees only the client and product information on the accounts he or she is handling.

- **Deliver customer profile information.** The system will be able to deliver the specific client and product information that representatives need at a specific time so that when they walk into a customer's business, they are armed with exactly the information they need, which will make them more productive. Account managers can manage customer and partner relationships better, tailor discussions with customers based on sales analytics, and be more efficient with their time by delivering targeted messages to accounts. The system determines the most appropriate content to provide to a given user in a given context, based on information stored in the database.

- **Provide specific sales opportunities based on customer profiles.** Your sales representative can be armed with information on product lines and sell-through rates, effectiveness of discounts and seasonal specials, billing or invoicing data, calls to customer help desks or inventory control clerks, and offers for upcoming products or deep discounts for soon-to-be-discontinued product lines. They can be kept up to date on the latest releases and product offerings, and can give customers the ability to buy or preorder the newest products on the market.

- **Generate sales reports.** Targeting tools can also be used to generate sales reports for retail representatives, including information on commissions, returns, quota achievement, or bonus opportunity progress.

These tools can also be used for customized client reports or for the customers themselves. You can market them as a free or cost-plus service. Information on order status, open trouble tickets, special promotions, or discounts can be given to customers, perhaps on a subscription basis, or you can provide them with information sources such as white papers or newsletters. The content of the newsletters should vary based on user profile: employees and clients will each receive versions customized to their needs and interests. This data is fed back into the system so that the effectiveness of marketing programs, coupons, and discounts can be used to generate the next round of targeted marketing information. The system continually evaluates and refines itself, allowing you to easily fine-tune existing programs and discontinue ineffective ones. This is an example of how advanced information management can help close the loop between customer behavior and sales and marketing tactics.

Customer Self-Service and Management Applications

Customers have grown familiar with shopping cart applications on the Internet; in fact, most expect some kind of online shopping experience that lets them purchase goods and services online. However, it's one thing to offer a list of goods or services, and another one entirely to offer customization or build-to-order applications. For businesses that offer more than just a shopping mall experience and seek to offer a truly customized user experience, online retail Web applications can provide this service to customers. Smart Web pages and well-designed applications become sophisticated self-service Web sites, empowering customers by arming them with the right information and giving them the opportunity to conduct their own form of "what if" analysis: What will these options look like? What will the cost be? How do shipping options change the final total? This leads to improved customer satisfaction and customer loyalty over the long haul.

These sites are also convenient for exposing catalog information to suppliers, partners, and distributors. These "customers" also have a need for product and service information and the ability to analyze data quickly. Channel partners may want to adjust shipping quantities on the fly or separate or combine orders to improve their ability to do business with their clients. For instance, instead of waiting for all 50 widgets to be in stock before shipping, a channel partner may elect to have the 15 widgets in stock ship immediately and have the remainder filled at a later time. If these services are offered to your nonretail customers, you dramatically improve your ability to continue doing business with them and lessen the chance of losing them because of dissatisfaction with order processing.

Expanding Internet Presence with Transactional Capabilities

Retailers might use one or more systems to plan, budget, and forecast for the week, month, and year, and a completely different set of systems and software to order and obtain products from numerous suppliers. Legacy systems might be employed to send advance-shipping notices to stores, track product shipment, and facilitate the division of the product into quantities suitable for sale. Decision support systems might be used to create on-the-fly programs for placing a product so that it sells quicker or fits the buying patterns of specific customers. Dumb terminals might be used to finalize sales, while back-office tasks such as sales auditing, reconciliation, loss prevention, and labor scheduling are performed on personal computers.

Somehow all these systems must be tied together. Suddenly awareness strikes—many of these systems are transactional. *Transactional systems* are commonly associated with mainframes or other glass-house, high-end hardware and operating systems. Many of these are mission critical, running 24/7, using complex protocols for exchanging messages and data, such as guaranteed delivery, transaction rollback, and security. These systems are most commonly found in order-entry or banking applications but can be found anywhere there is a need for the highest levels of application integrity.

A retail Web site can act as the front end to transactional systems and can participate in these systems, including complex ones that involve activity within multiple systems using multipart transactions. This participation can include improved B2B and business-to-commerce (B2C) support, multiple purchase orders per order group, multiple shipments per purchase order, or support for shipping methods and tax rates. These can invoke several different transactions within several different systems, all of which must succeed together as a group to be committed or put into action. Retail Web sites with this support can be used to quickly implement and configure order-processing functionality, including the integration of third-party plug-in components for shipping, gift certificates, payment processing, and tax calculation. If individuals in a call center are handling this, the order process could conceivably take half an hour to an hour per order; with support for transactional systems, the order entry time is cut dramatically, leading to more orders processed and more revenue generated.

Shifting Implementation from Development to Marketing

In an ideal world, developers would not need to make content changes in a retail Web site. Product managers, without waiting for weeks for others to make changes, would handle common tasks such as deploying new product information, sales and promotional information, other content in general, and online sales capabilities. Progress has been made toward that goal, and much of it is available in a retail Web solution with advanced baseline capabilities.

In building on the business analytics and targeted marketing capabilities present in advanced Internet technology, retail Web sites empower business managers to act on business intelligence without involving developers or IT staff. For example, product managers can generate and deploy their own marketing or product campaigns based on almost instant customer feedback. They are allowed to quickly define a unique product catalog and manage the creation of categories that match their products. Product managers can then operate this tool through a simple Web-based graphical user interface (GUI), allowing business users to perform common business operations, including reviewing reports, creating marketing campaigns, updating product data, and modifying profiles. This reduces both the time and cost involved in updating the site in response to trends or market conditions; business users can react to market changes and market dynamics faster, leading to a strengthened competitive advantage and improved ability to shape the way a company does business.

Developers, in turn, are freed from day-to-day site maintenance to focus on more substantive development tasks, such as more complex features, application integration, or upgrade issues. Powerful base technology in retail Web sites greatly streamlines the development process by providing complete basic functionality, on which a site is built. Ease of programmability enables the development team to implement custom features and deploy the storefront and robust supporting systems very quickly. In addition, future business endeavors will benefit from even faster deployment, as they leverage the platform and architecture.

Improving Manageability

A full-featured retail Web site dramatically reduces administration by consolidating the required technical skill sets. A business no longer needs separate, full-time database administrators to perform common tasks like updating the inventory information or maintaining catalog content. Instead it empowers business managers to modify the database with catalog content, business analytics, and targeted marketing campaigns, further reducing the burden on IT staff and resulting in greater cost savings and more timely and effective targeting of customers. It enables IT staff to focus more effectively on other technical challenges that arise in the course of business, making them more efficient, and providing them with more resources to accomplish more in the long run. Work is distributed across the organization to where it makes sense, reducing the likelihood of any one group being a significant bottleneck.

Administering this powerful code base can seem like the lesser of two evils when compared with the prospect of upgrading whole enterprises or migrating all of your business processes to one platform. However, if you want to be successful in the new economy and take advantage of emerging trends such as online ordering, self-checkouts, wireless registry systems, and customer price verifiers, you must consider either deploying your development staff to rewrite code to run on legacy systems or investing your entire IT budget in brand new systems and software. The retail Web site offers a third alternative: creating a middle ground, where the Web site interoperates with your existing business systems, yet provides significantly lower administrative costs by shifting tasks to where they make sense. Your IT staff will continue to maintain hardware and networking investments, monitor server performance, and balance workloads. Your business managers will create marketing campaigns, update Web content and catalog content, and deploy new marketing programs without requiring IT's involvement.

Smart companies seeking both long-term and short-term benefits and returns on investment would be wise to consider implementing a retail Internet presence, complete with advanced tools and technology that allow product managers to manage their product lines and allow developers to concentrate on code base design and development.

Summary

This chapter focused on the additional technical challenges and innovations present in managing a retail Internet presence. These sites require sophisticated data handling and analysis capabilities, along with integrated reporting and content management technologies that allow business managers to "close the loop" in response to customer actions. In the next chapter, you'll see how the Microsoft Solutions Framework ties all the pieces together, using both advanced technology and service professionals to create powerful Internet solutions for businesses.

Microsoft Frameworks

The success of IT implementation projects can typically be traced back to basic adherence to a planning and deployment methodology. When projects fail the reason is rarely technical, because Internet solutions require contributions from a team of both internal and external resources. In fact, Allie Young in *Outsourcing Service Opportunities* (Dataquest, 1999) found that more than 70 percent of customers are turning to external service providers for some aspects of their IT deployments. Microsoft Solution for Internet Business is no exception. That is, a customer seeking Microsoft Solution for Internet Business implementation expertise would most likely turn to an external service provider with that specific expertise.

Microsoft offers three enterprise services frameworks for providing technology solutions: Microsoft Readiness Framework (MRF), Microsoft Solutions Framework (MSF), and Microsoft Operations Framework (MOF). As a general rule, enterprises are defined as large organizations (size estimates vary, but they generally have more than 1000 users) or organizations that, although small in size, have characteristics of large organizations (for example, very heavy Web traffic in a retail environment). These frameworks are Microsoft's answer to the market's need for methodologies to meet critical technology goals. The framework goals are to drive process improvement throughout the organization with goals of higher software quality, lower development and maintenance costs, shorter time to market, and increased predictability and controllability of software products to market.

Each of the three frameworks is focused on different integral phases of the Internet solution life cycle. This specialization allows each framework to supply useful and detailed information on team organization, processes, and technologies for a specific phase's success. Note that detailed information on these frameworks can be obtained from Microsoft's Web site at *www.microsoft.com* and other Microsoft resources such as the subscription-based TechNet. In fact, this chapter refers to these same resources, including white papers dedicated to each separate methodology. The three frameworks are defined as follows:

- **MRF.** This is the preparation phase for the Internet solution project. The MRF has four key upstream integrated phases: planning, assessing, changing, and evaluation. Planning is about what you want, assessing is about what you have, changing is about how to get there, and evaluation is about whether you are done.

- **MSF.** MSF provides guidance in the planning, building, and deploying phases of the project life cycle of Internet solutions. Such guidance includes white papers, deployment guides, case studies, and courseware in the areas of enterprise architecture, application development, component design, and infrastructure deployment.

- **MOF.** The MOF offers comprehensive technical guidance for achieving mission-critical production system reliability, availability, and manageability on Microsoft's products and technologies. This guidance takes the form of white papers, operational guides, assessment tools, best practices, case studies, and support tools for effective data center management within today's complex distributed IT environment.

The big picture involving MRF, MSF, and MOF is this: MRF enables the organization to determine its organizational readiness. The resulting readiness plan is used over the course of the project. MSF and MOF then follow the traditional IT life cycle from start to finish, with MSF handling the planning and building technology solutions and MOF managing these solutions on a day-to-day basis. MRF, MSF, and MOF, as shown in Figure 8-1, are defined in greater detail in the following sections, so you will learn how these frameworks function together. For the purpose of the Internet solutions discussion, the main focus of this chapter is MSF and MOF. MSF is the approach most closely aligned with implementation projects. MOF is used for the operations and maintenance of a working Microsoft Solution for Internet Business site.

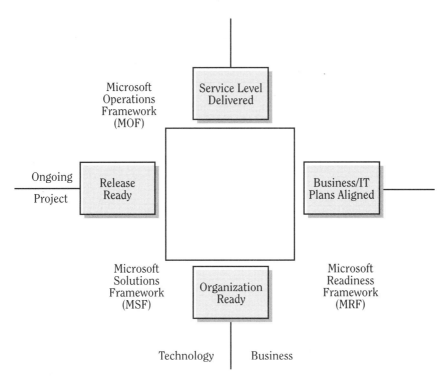

Figure 8-1. *Microsoft frameworks.*

In this chapter, we define MRF, MSF, and MOF and explore the relationship among these frameworks and how they affect the Microsoft Solution for Internet Business.

Microsoft Readiness Framework

Although the MRF could be introduced at any stage of a project, it typically is most useful before starting or in the early planning stages when an organization is evaluating a new technology. In the context of Internet solutions, MRF helps customer IT organizations and Microsoft partners identify and develop the sufficient level of organizational readiness needed to introduce the Internet solution into the company environment, including the business practices. The delivery of MRF entails activities geared toward getting ready for new technology, including getting ready to plan, build, or manage that technology. To reiterate, MRF specifically deals with organizational readiness.

Organizational Readiness

Organizational readiness is the state of an organization with regard to the alignment of business objectives, IT plans, and organizational competencies. Establishing business objectives entails having a clear vision and powerful business case for what the business will achieve. Once objectives are defined, a company must look at what business processes must be in place to support these objectives. Aligning IT plans is the next step—in particular, understanding how and what technology can support and accelerate these business processes. Understanding what organizational competencies (knowledge, skills, abilities, and behavior) are needed to support business objectives and IT plans is pivotal to enabling these two factors. The focus is on the readiness cycle, including planning the desired future state, assessing an organization's current state, changing an organization to support the future state, and evaluating the impact of these changes.

The six key organizational indicators of an organization's readiness are as follows:

- Culture
- Leadership
- Skills
- Process
- Hardware
- Software

Culture and leadership represent the organization's intent or capability to create change. Skills and process represent the organization's capability to execute that change. Hardware and software represent the catalysts for the change and the most tangible products of the technology change.

Individual Readiness

Individual readiness is the state of an IT professional with regard to the technical competencies, skills, and proficiency levels required to use the technologies and products in planning, building, and managing technology solutions (such as Internet solutions). Although anyone in an organization can benefit from MRF, its primary consumers are the IT, training, and business managers responsible for the readiness of their organizations. Such individuals include the enterprise IT managers and professionals as well as the consulting organizations that need to plan, build, and manage Internet solutions based on Microsoft platforms.

MRF Principles

MRF is designed to address the dynamic, volatile nature of technology environments, including organizations introducing Internet solutions. The following business and technology principles on which MRF is based are fundamental to its design and successful application:

- **Business/IT/organizational alignment.** It is critical to the successful adoption of any new technology that the IT goals are aligned with the business goals and organizational capabilities, regardless of whether the technology is driving new opportunities for the business or supporting existing lines of business.

- **Continuous process improvement.** This is a multifaceted concern: readiness, learning, and training are fundamentally part of a life cycle that is not attached to a single event, but must occur at every phase of a project and throughout the life cycle of the technology.

- **Planning.** A core element of a project's success, readiness must be considered early in project planning to minimize risk and maximize resources.

- **Best practices.** To augment the application, proven industry best practices in both technology and change implementation are leveraged and Microsoft platform best practices are provided.

- **Measurement.** There is an old adage that you cannot manage what you cannot measure. This truth lies at the heart of MRF. Utilizing assessments and milestones helps ensure that the customer is achieving the desired return on investment (ROI).

- **Customer focus.** Focusing efforts on what the customer is trying to achieve will bring about the most success.

- **Executive sponsorship and management commitment.** It is critical that management demonstrate commitment, leadership, and involvement in the process through the clear communication of purpose and goals. The organization and the individuals within the organization must be willing to make the investment—both in dollars and time—to integrate the change, or the project will fail.

- **Managing change.** Change is an inevitable part of any project. Therefore, managing change successfully is crucial to the success of the project.

MRF Process Model

The MRF process model takes the form of an iterative life cycle comprising four integrated phases, each of which has both organizational and individual activities. The MRF process model can be applied equally to broad-scale technology projects and projects with a more limited scope.

Each phase ends with a key milestone that must be achieved before the next phase can begin. The milestone determines the activities that occur within the next phase, and the phases are designed to move the project team from one to the next in a logical fashion. Table 8-1 lists the four phases along with the key objective for the business decision maker (BDM) and the key milestone of each phase.

Table 8-1. MRF Process Model

Phase	Objective	Phase Milestone
Planning	Define what you want: Align the business goals, IT goals, and organizational capabilities to create a shared vision of what the organization will look like when this process is complete.	Capabilities and competencies map, defined as: **Organizational level:** Future organization capabilities identified. **Individual level:** Individual scenarios produced, occupational clusters mapped to team roles, competency lists produced, and proficiency levels identified.

Table 8-1. **MRF Process Model** *(continued)*

Phase	Objective	Phase Milestone
Assessing	Determine what you have: Through assessment and review, determine what competencies and capabilities exist within the organization today.	Gap analysis. The primary steps for performing a gap analysis are: 1. Identify the gap between the way employees work today and how you want them to work when the deployment is complete. 2. Computers and operating systems are only of value to your business if they are of value to your employees. A successful deployment closes the gap between the way employees work today and the way the new system will empower them to work when the deployment is complete. Later, when the team begins to measure the rate of success, the primary measure will be how it has improved the work of those who are using the system. 3. Review documents, if any, from previous computer and network upgrades. In addition to providing useful information about the current computing environment, existing documents can provide a template to follow as you move through the decision-making process. 4. Review documents obtained from hardware or software vendors. Documents that relate to the current hardware and software in your infrastructure will help you decide whether to upgrade or replace computing resources. 5. Identify tasks and determine resource requirements for each one. After you have identified the tasks and determined what resources are required to accomplish them, you can determine which groups within the organization need to be involved and whether you will need additional resources from outside the organization. 6. Update any documents such as spreadsheets or schedules with planning, work, and resource assignments. Keeping documents updated will make it easier to plan work schedules and allocate resources. 7. Send the gap analysis documents to the appropriate decision makers in your organization for approval. If approval is granted, then the project can begin; if not, you need to make changes to the documents and put them through the approval process again before you begin implementation.

continued

Table 8-1.   MRF Process Model   *(continued)*

Phase	Objective	Phase Milestone
Changing	Through change and learning, transition what you have into what you want, bridging the gap defined in the first two phases.	Readiness review, defined as a capabilities development plan and cost model (time allocation for training, outsourcing versus recruiting).
Evaluating	Determine whether you have achieved your objectives and integrate the organizational learning back into the collective consciousness of the organization to make the next project more successful.	Organizational readiness, defined as a final readiness review. For the individual, the deliverable might be obtaining technical certification.

The four phases of the MRF model are displayed in Figure 8-2.

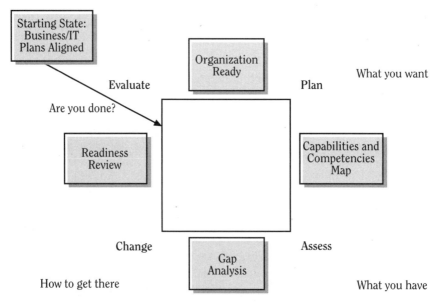

Figure 8-2.   *The four phases of the MRF model.*

Microsoft Solutions Framework

The MSF is really a collection of methodologies whereby you select the best of breed model from several MSF models that fit your particular situation. These individual models, each of which is discussed in the following sections, are as follows:

- **Team model.** Build high-performance teams.

- **Process model.** Make better development trade-offs.

- **Application model.** Design for flexibility.

- **Solutions design model.** Anticipate user needs.

- **Enterprise architecture model.** Integrate the business.

- **Infrastructure model.** Deploy systems better.

- **Total cost of ownership model.** Identify and lower cost factors.

Team Model

Experience has shown that technology implementations, be it software development or the deployment of an Internet solution, take on certain common characteristics. In these cases it is essential that synergy be created so the team is much more than just a group of people assigned to the same project. It is important that the team, to be effective, has the correct skill sets and specializations for the project, empowers members to use that expertise, and holds members accountable for results in their respective ownership areas. In particular, accountability and empowerment remove the obstacles to high achievement.

A common technology team model has the following roles, which can easily be defined for an Internet solution deployment project.

- **Product management.** This role is multifaceted. The incumbent articulates a vision for the product or service, defines customer requirements (including the management of customer expectations), and develops and maintains the business case for the technology solution.

- **Program management.** The individuals in this role drive the critical decisions necessary to release the solution (for example, an Internet solution) at the right time. This includes coordinating the required decisions to deliver the solution in a manner consistent with organizational standards and interoperability goals.

- **Development.** This team builds or implements a product or service that fully meets and complies with the project specifications and customer expectations.

- **Testing.** The individuals in the testing area ensure all issues are known before the release of the solution (in this case, an Internet solution).

- **User education.** The goal of this team is to maximize the user experience through performance solutions and training systems. A key goal is to reduce support costs by increasing the usability of the solution.

- **Logistics.** This group ensures a smooth rollout, installation, and migration of the solution.

There are several tangible benefits to the team model. It gives each member a stake in the success of the solution. It creates a culture that encourages clarity, efficiency, participation, commitment, and team spirit. Accountability is improved, as is the overall customer focus of the solution.

Process Model

The process model has two possible outcomes, one positive and one negative: bringing order to operations and becoming focused on study rather than action. The process model is good for keeping operations focused and on track. Lack of a process model can result in a firefighting mentality in which everything is urgent. Tired team members lose focus because they are distracted by chronic issues. Paralysis of analysis is the other possible outcome, in which little meaningful work occurs, but much study does. There is a balance between the two and therein lies the challenge of the process model.

When an effective process model is lacking, obstacles to success can include the following:

- The project morphed into something it wasn't initially designed to be.

- The project is taking too long and is becoming too expensive.

- Feature creep at or near the release date creates delays.

- A showstopper or major issue has been discovered, forcing a project restart.

- Even though the project is completed and on time, it isn't needed any more by the organization.

The process model is composed of four phases, as shown in Figure 8-3: envisioning, planning, developing, and stabilization.

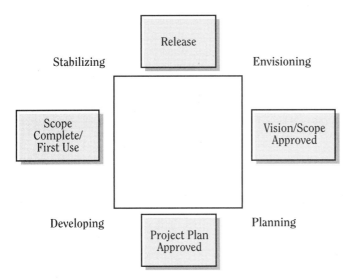

Figure 8-3. *Four phases of the process model.*

Envisioning

In its most pure form, envisioning keeps an organization from investing substantial effort in meeting minor needs or making dysfunctional processes more efficient. This forward-thinking step requires open-minded participants to think about how a proposed solution addresses both current and future needs. The vision or scope approved milestone is the desired outcome of the envisioning phase. A vision statement articulates the goals for the Internet solution and provides clear direction. Conversely, the scope is much more limiting and it defines boundaries for what the Internet solution can and cannot deliver. Current limitations are typically an opportunity for a future release as a new feature set.

Planning

Simply stated, planning involves the stakeholders in an Internet solution agreeing on what is to be delivered and when. The project planning approved milestone is the desired outcome of this phase. The project plan contains the functional specification and the project schedule. The functional specification provides the project team with sufficient detail to identify resource requirements and make commitments.

Note   Project planning is discussed in *Chapter 9, "Project Management."*

Developing

The primary outcome from the developing phase is the scope complete and first use milestone. This is an approved functional specification and project plan that provides the baseline for focused development on the Internet solution to begin. The customer and team assess the Internet solution's functionality and verify that rollout and support plans are in place.

Stabilizing

This phase is a paradigm shift from creativity to structured operations, culminating in the release milestone. Bugs are fixed as the primary focus, and then the Internet solution is officially turned over to the operations and support groups. At this time, the project team is dispersed.

The process model differs from traditional models in the following ways:

- Vision and scope are emphasized rather than requirements.

- Customer-oriented milestones are emphasized rather than development-centered milestones. Each milestone is a synchronization point where the team is recalibrated to customer expectations. Trade-offs among resources, features, and schedules are made to manage milestones as appropriate.

- Releases are versioned rather than trying to have the first release of an Internet solution contain all features. This allows the rapid delivery of the Internet solution with a plan for improvement.

The process model results in better decisions, less rework, higher morale, and a higher quality product.

Application Model

The conventional thinking today, in the early twenty-first century, is that applications have a clear division between user interface (UI), business rules, and data. This logical division of an application allows significant flexibility in adapting the UI over time or applying business rules to new data sources. In the application model there are essentially two camps: traditional and services views.

Traditional View

This application viewpoint is vertical, eliminating the economies of scale that could be achieved by linking application design, infrastructure usage, and component reuse across functional departments.

Services View

A service is a unit of application logic that implements an operation, function, or transformation that is applied to an object. Services can enforce business rules; perform calculations or manipulations on data; and expose features for entering, reviewing, viewing, or modifying information. There are three categories of services that strive for efficiency (such as reuse of development assets):

- **User services.** This provides the UI for the user.

- **Business services.** This controls business rules. Business services transform data into information through the appropriate application of business rules.

- **Data services.** This is the lowest visible level of abstraction used for the manipulation of data. Data services maintain the availability and integrity of persistent and nonpersistent data. This includes create, read, update, and delete capabilities such that the business services do not need to know where the data is located, how it is implemented, or how it is accessed.

The services viewpoint is particularly applicable as business systems are integrated with Internet technologies for the following reasons:

- They provide a consistent UI style and navigation model for all business applications.

- They establish and maintain a presence on the Web.

- They simplify the deployment of applications through the centralized maintenance of application logic on an Internet server.

Solutions Design Model

One of the key factors in designing a successful business solution is the consideration for, and involvement of, users throughout the design process. Unfortunately, user involvement in development projects can be difficult to manage. Development organizations give the following common reasons for not involving users:

- The users don't know what they want beyond what is in their current system.

- Users are resistant to change. They don't want the new technology and will not get involved in its design.

- Users have different opinions of what the new system should include and have different preferences for the UI.

- Users ask for a feature, but when it is delivered they want something different.

However, without a clear perspective on day-to-day use of the system, certain obstacles to success are predictable. Perhaps you've witnessed some of these symptoms in your own projects:

- The project is underway, but users have already solved the problem in several different ways.

- The project is almost complete, but it might create more workflow problems than it solves.

- The application specifications aren't changing, but the business is, and you can't track with it.

- The project solves many of your infrastructure problems, but people refuse to use it.

- The application is complete, but high help-desk costs make a full deployment doubtful.

This model helps prevent these obstacles by relating solutions development to the goals of the business in two key ways:

- **User involvement.** Solutions are driven from the context of the business, an essential consideration when developing workflow applications. End users are brought in to address usability before incurring help-desk incidents. IT professionals are brought in before end users solve their own problems without addressing infrastructure.

- **Iterative, sequential development.** Three perspectives—conceptual, logical, and physical—help planners identify all business and technical requirements of an application up front for better assignment of resources. These perspectives are discussed in the following sections.

Conceptual

The design of an Internet solution starts with the information architect's vision. This view corresponds to the conceptual design for the project. This starting point is an understanding of what the users really need to do and the creation of an easily communicated set of models that captures this understanding.

Logical

The information architect's vision is followed by plans, showing the Internet solution as seen by the architect and contributing staff, often in the form of a storyboard. This second phase in the architectural process combines the customer's view with the information architect's view and knowledge, providing detailed plans in each of many categories for communication with the different consultants and solution providers involved in the project. This corresponds to the logical design, where the structure and communication among the individual elements of a system are laid out.

Physical

Finally, plans are drawn up as specifications, adding detail to the information architect's plans, making adjustments for the technology and materials available to build the Internet solution. This view directs all the development activities and corresponds to the physical design, where the real-world constraints of technology, including implementation and performance considerations, are applied to the logical model. This is the point at which real resources, costs, and schedules can be estimated.

Think of these three perspectives on design as convenient points along a continuum to apply a particular set of techniques and tools and address the needs of a particular audience. This enables us to describe the design process in a more focused way. At any given point, portions of the design can be revisited, as design is a continuing process of successive refinement.

Enterprise Architecture Model

Enterprise architecture planning in many ways resembles urban planning. Urban planners plan and develop an infrastructure to deliver utilities and services that support a wide range of activities in various types of communities. As the population and the economy grow, the infrastructure requires periodic improvements to accommodate users. The same applies to enterprise architecture. Enterprise architects plan for the necessary infrastructures, utilities, systems, and processes that business applications use to access and exchange critical information throughout the organization. Infrastructure development and management activities represent the public works necessary to support growth.

If this periodic improvement to the infrastructure does not happen, certain divisions are predictable between old and new technologies or between technology and the business. Perhaps you've seen some of these symptoms in your own projects:

- You can't define new technical guidelines because you're still supporting legacy systems.

- Every time you define a set of corporate standards, the technology changes.

- You know where the technology needs to lead, but departments keep rebelling.

- You're too busy just keeping everything running to stop and look ahead.

- Managing was tough enough with your assets in one room, but now they're spread all over the world.

In general, enterprise architecture planning takes place continuously as business needs evolve, and it has earned the reputation as "planning while building." It uses such approaches as risk-driven scheduling, a fixed release date mindset, activity-based planning, visible milestones, and small teams. Architecture planning parallels, and ultimately sustains, ongoing solution development projects. In contrast to top-down methods, projects not only are driven by an enterprise model, they directly affect the evolution of the enterprise architecture.

To make this happen, the enterprise architecture model provides a consistent set of guidelines for planning, building, and managing a technology infrastructure. It encompasses four perspectives: business, application, information, and technology. Visualizing each perspective enables you to develop better change-management strategies for your enterprise.

Business Architecture

Business architecture describes how the business works. It describes the functions and the cross-functional activities an organization performs. The process of describing the business architecture highlights opportunities to use technology to increase revenue, decrease expenses, or enhance innovation. The business architecture helps establish boundaries for clear requirements and development of vision and scope for each project. Key questions you might ask are:

- What industry is your business in?

- What services and resources are required to run your business?

- What are your core strengths?

- What trends affect your business?

- Is your market expanding or contracting?

- Where will your industry be in five years?

- How are your margins?

- Do your core processes meet customers' needs?

- Will new systems have a positive effect on cash flow, revenue, or expenses?

Application Architecture

The application architecture describes the standard interfaces, services, and application models needed by the business. These translate into development resources for the project teams (for example, component and code libraries, standards documents, design guidelines). It describes the automated services that support the business processes depicted in the business architecture, and it describes the interaction and interdependencies of the organization's applications. Also, it provides guidelines for developing new applications and moving to new application models. There are several important questions you might ask:

- What are your integration issues with current application systems?

- What application models do you use within your organization?

- Where are your application backlogs?

- Which applications are unique to your business?

- Which applications could best be bought from independent software vendors?

- Do you prefer cutting-edge solutions or lean toward stability?

- Do your core applications inhibit customer service?

Information Architecture

The information architecture describes what the organization needs to know to run its business processes and operations. It includes standard data models, data management policies, and descriptions of the patterns of information consumption and production in the organization. It describes how data is bound into the workflow, documents, and personal files that pervade the organization. Some of the most critical information resides not just in database servers but also on the thousands of desktops that abound in most enterprises. Consider the following questions:

- What does the business need to know?

- What are the industry requirements and standards?

- What are your critical information needs?

- What are your biggest data issues?

- What are your functional data requirements?

- What are your business process data and workflow requirements?

- Are there statutory or legal constraints that affect your data and information needs?

Technology Architecture

The technology architecture lays out standards and guidelines for the acquisition and deployment of client and workstation tools, application building blocks, infrastructure services, network connectivity components, and platforms. Acquisition entails build-or-buy decisions, and deployment entails developing technology blueprints to guide the evolution of the technology infrastructure. Ask the following questions:

- What level of technology risk can you accept?

- Do you deploy approved, standard technologies or buy ad hoc?

- Do you understand how, what, and where technology is deployed in your organization?

- Does your technology infrastructure map to your business needs?

- What are the key technology trends affecting your IT operations?

- Do you know what technical skills you need today and tomorrow?

Together, these four perspectives—business, application, information, and technology—help your organization plan while building, turning each business-driven project into a further evolution of your enterprise architecture. This allows new technology to steadily drive your business toward a competitive advantage.

Infrastructure Model

Infrastructure means different things to different people. A software developer might identify infrastructure as the software elements that work within a computing environment. A hardware engineer might assume that infrastructure is the physical elements that form the network. An individual with a human resources background might identify infrastructure with personnel and services performed. All of them would be correct. The computing infrastructure is a composite of all these elements, and more.

MSF defines infrastructure as the total set of resources necessary to support the enterprise computing environment. These resources consist of the technologies and standards (as identified in the enterprise architecture), the operational processes (policies, operating procedures, and services), and the people and organizational resources (skill sets and management).

If infrastructure is not deployed well, certain obstacles to success are predictable. Consider the following symptoms in infrastructure projects:

- Important business projects are on hold until underlying technology issues are resolved.

- New technology must be evaluated, but no criteria exist for making decisions.

- User mobility is increasing the time spent administering security policies.

- The project is being rolled out when the help desk discovers it can't be supported.

- The deployment timeline is being determined by whether or not the application works as planned.

A project that takes more than one year to complete might lose its value because of the rapid rate at which technology is evolving. On large projects, for example, the deployment of any single version of technology might never be complete. As soon as one wave of deployment is nearing completion, another wave will be in the planning stages. To achieve this, the customer and project team must collaborate to prioritize and make trade-off decisions on the three project management parameters: schedule, scope, and resources. Another possibility is to fast track a project by "crashing," or allocating mass quantities of resources (for example, doubling or tripling the size of the project team).

The infrastructure model applies the roles, functions, and expectations of the process model and team model to the requirements of rolling out a successful infrastructure, achieving a dual purpose. First, established best practices are applied to a complex operation, increasing its chance for success. Second, those on the team reuse familiar knowledge, helping your organization do more in less time with fewer people.

When applying Microsoft's process model to infrastructure projects, some labels are changed to emphasize the specific characteristics of this type of project. For example, the developing phase in the basic model becomes the fulfillment phase in deployment. This enables it to apply the core activities of envisioning, planning, developing, and stabilizing to an iterative deployment environment.

Who implements this process? The core roles defined earlier in the team model are still valid, own the same views of the project, and have the same types of interactions. However, to expand the model for an infrastructure deployment project, the six team roles are expanded with wider responsibilities, and the following three new areas are added to the logistics role:

- **System management.** Maintains accountability of the systems, technology, and continued operation of the technology.
- **Help desk.** Provides ongoing support to the user.
- **Communications.** Maintains voice, video, and data communications capabilities.

The end result of the infrastructure model is a more flexible approach to technology deployment that gets new technology in place and delivering value in less time. If your team is already familiar with the team and process models, this is a highly effective way to reuse that knowledge to benefit the organization.

Total Cost of Ownership Model

The idea behind the total cost of ownership (TCO) model is simple: reduce costs to get a better return on the technology investment. What rational BDM wouldn't want to spend less?

A closer examination of the issue, however, reveals that it is not as simplistic as it appears. Consider the following:

- **The role of value.** It's possible to reduce your TCO to zero by eliminating all computers from the organization, along with any competitive advantage they bring. This extreme view highlights two key points—that value must be part of the equation, and that the overall goal isn't really minimizing TCO but optimizing TCO against the value that is unique to each organization. Clearly, eliminating computers from an organization isn't a realistic option today with the reliance on data processing and technology solutions.

- **What is really a cost?** There are a variety of TCO models in the industry, with annual costs per desktop PC ranging from $3,200 to $13,000. This discrepancy is caused by a lack of agreement about what soft and fully loaded costs are included in a good TCO analysis. Microsoft offers a comprehensive model to help organizations understand the cost of owning and using each IT component over time.

- **Applying TCO to your needs.** Some TCO models include a large percentage for fully loaded costs of undefined end-user activities. This approach makes accurate costs hard to measure, substantiate, and apply to your own organization in a useful way.

- **Seeing the whole picture.** Some vendors treat TCO primarily as an acquisition cost, creating entire new classes of devices that transfer the acquisition cost to the network, development, and other cost areas.

However, without a measurable, customizable model for identifying and managing costs, certain obstacles to success are predictable. Some of these symptoms in an organization are:

- You know that your costs are high but don't know what to do about it.

- You think that your costs are high but have no way of comparing them to any reliable benchmark.

- Your move to less expensive equipment has been matched by the increasing cost of complexity.

- You switched to distributed computing for more flexibility, but now the variety of platforms supported is hindering your ability to deliver cost-effective flexible solutions.

- You're evaluating new technology with total cost in mind, but you won't know how cost relates to the decision until after you have deployed the technology.

TCO is a continual process of ongoing improvement with three key stages: planning, building, and managing. This approach can be useful in developing business cases and priorities for infrastructure projects.

Planning

In the planning phase, the model provides direction to calculate benchmarks, cost baselines, ROIs, and validation. The benchmark is a determination of total costs based on industry average costs. A baseline report is a determination of the actual costs of acquiring, managing, and retiring network-based technology assets.

Building

In the building phase, ROI is calculated by simulating the impact of recommended improvement projects and cost savings over time based on a particular migration and deployment strategy.

Managing

The managing phase measures actual results against the objectives established, validating or invalidating the TCO optimization strategy.

This life-cycle approach optimizes the following technology cost areas:

- **Hardware and software.** Desktop hardware and software, servers, routers, bridges, and upgrades

- **Support.** Maintenance, disaster recovery, help desk, administration, and training

- **Development.** Code and content development

- **Management.** Network, systems, and data management

- **End-user costs.** Cooperative end-user training, peer support, and general "futzing" with the PC

- **Downtime/other.** Planned and unplanned downtime, applications development, and testing

- **Telecommunications fees.** Leased lines and other communications expenses

Most important, the majority of costs are not found in the acquisition of hardware and software but in the labor needed to develop, support, and maintain an IT infrastructure. Optimizing these costs requires a combination of the best use of technology, skilled IT resources, and best practices.

For instance, it is common to find organizations failing to take advantage of system policies, logon scripts, and user profiles in today's technology. Overcoming this requires education. Other useful best practices include well-defined asset management procedures, standard common operating environments, and training.

A comprehensive TCO strategy entails measurement and improvements to the people, process, and technology elements of the enterprise. IT infrastructure processes (network operations, network and data management, administration, help desk) should be as efficient and effective as possible. In contrast, the end user should be as self-sufficient as possible, as the goal is to reduce user utilization of IT infrastructure processes.

The benefits of the MSF TCO model are proven in organizations that have applied it, including Microsoft. Optimize your TCO around the value you need from Microsoft technology. An MSF expert can help you adapt this model to your specific needs.

More than anything else, MSF is about developing a culture of excellence, devoted to passionate expression of ideas, implementation of a shared vision, and ongoing improvement. The rewards are huge, leading to better business solutions developed in less time by fewer people.

However, cultural change is not easy. It requires commitment at all levels. Front-line workers must be ready to communicate as peers and cross-organizational boundaries. Senior executives must be ready to drive the organizational changes that allow cross-functional integration to happen and act as sponsors to high-profile projects.

Realistically, sending lots of people to a training class won't change a corporate culture (except possibly for attitudes toward training). But measurable best practices with milestones, delivered in the context of an actual project by an experienced consultant, can be applied effectively to achieve successful results. Nothing drives cultural change like success. Organizations that successfully make the cultural shift with MSF continue to enjoy highly capable teams long after the initial project ends.

If your organization is ready to commit to change, or you would like to start building this commitment in your organization now, ask an MSF certified trainer for a presentation and demonstration. You'll see how this set of best practices can be applied to your specific needs for planning, building, or managing technology-driven business solutions.

Microsoft Operations Framework

MOF is a collection of best practices, principles, and models. It provides comprehensive technical guidance for achieving mission-critical production system reliability, availability, supportability, and manageability using Microsoft's products and technologies. MOF is one of the three frameworks that form the Microsoft frameworks (the other two are the MRF and MSF discussed earlier in this chapter). Each targets a different, but integral, phase in the IT life cycle. Each framework provides useful and detailed information on the people, processes, and technologies required to successfully execute within its respective area.

MOF Overview

Delivering the high levels of reliability and availability that business-to-consumer (B2C) Web sites need requires not only great technology but also proven operational processes. Microsoft has built on industry experience and best practices to create the knowledge base required to set up and run these processes. The MOF framework is based on two important concepts: service solutions and IT service management.

Service Solutions

Service solutions are the capabilities, or business functions, that IT provides to its customers. Examples of service solutions include:

- Application service provisioning
- E-commerce
- Messaging
- Knowledge management

Based on recent trends in application hosting and outsourcing, MOF strongly supports providing software as a service solution.

IT Service Management

IT service management consists of the functions that customers need to maintain a specific service solution. Examples of IT service management functions include:

- Help desk
- Problem management
- Contingency planning

MOF supports the use of well-defined service management functions to help IT operations provide business-focused service solutions. These service management functions provide consistent policies, procedures, standards, and best practices that can be applied across the entire suite of service solutions found in today's IT environments.

The MOF process model shown in Figure 8-4 shows where service management functions fit.

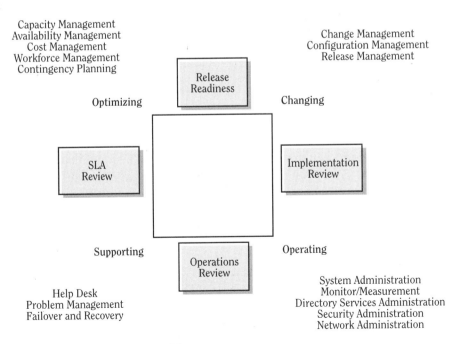

Figure 8-4. *MOF process model.*

MOF recognizes and even embraces the current industry best practice for IT service management that has been well documented within the Central Computer and Telecommunications Agency's (CCTA) IT Infrastructure Library (ITIL). The CCTA is a United Kingdom government executive agency chartered with development of best practice advice and guidance on the use of IT in service management and operations. To accomplish this, the CCTA charters projects with leading IT companies from around the world to document and validate best practices in the disciplines of IT service management.

MOF combines these collaborative industry standards with specific guidelines for running on the Microsoft platform in a variety of business scenarios. MOF extends the ITIL code of practice to support distributed IT environments and current industry directions such as application hosting, mobile device computing, and Web-based transactional and e-commerce systems.

Relating MOF to MSF

Additional elements of the MOF appear, at first glance, to be reiterations of the MSF model presented earlier in the chapter. These elements, although carrying the same title and content, are applied at different times, a point emphasized in the next section. Additional MOF elements include the process, team, and risk models.

Process Model

The process model for operations is a functional model of the processes that operations teams perform to manage and maintain IT services. The goal is to provide a simplified, more generalized way to look at complex IT environments. This model is based on four guiding principles:

- **Structured architecture.** The MOF process model is an architecture that structures all operational activities needed for mission-critical computing so that they are better able to deal with the increasingly complex environment.

- **Rapid life cycle, iterative improvement.** The rate of change for IT operations continues to accelerate. This demand for change is a direct response to the needs of business to adapt and innovate to stay competitive. As a result, MOF has incorporated the concept of an iterative life cycle that supports the abilities to incorporate change quickly and to continuously assess and improve the overall operations environment.

- **Review-driven management.** The process model includes reviews at key points in the life cycle in which the team evaluates performance for release-based activities as well as steady state, or daily operational activities. These major reviews let upper management get involved when their input is most needed.

- **Embedded risk management.** IT operations today are more important and more complex than ever before, and failures in operations are more visible to worldwide customers and users of IT. This means risk management in operations is crucial to ensure that operations does not fail the business.

Team Model

Under the team model, teams are organized into role clusters. The model then defines the key activities and competencies for each cluster. Guidance is provided on how to scale the team for projects of different sizes and different organization types. The guiding principles, listed here, advise individuals on how to run and operate distributed computing environments:

- To provide great customer service

- To understand the business priorities and enable IT to add business value

- To build strong, synergistic virtual teams

- To leverage IT automation and knowledge management tools

- To attract, develop, and retain strong IT operations staff

Risk Model

The risk model for operations applies proven risk management techniques to the problems that operations staff face every day. There are many models, frameworks, and processes for managing risks. They're all about planning for an uncertain future, and the risk model for operations is no exception. However, it offers greater value than many others through its key principles, a customized terminology, a structured and repeatable five-step process, and integration into a larger operations framework.

Origin

The risk model for operations was developed in response to customer requests for a framework to help organizations manage risk while running their businesses on the Microsoft platform. MSF defined a widely applicable risk model with a description that is customized to address risk management during projects, especially software development and deployment projects. The risk model for operations is based on the MSF risk model, with extensions and customizations to address the needs of operations groups.

Guiding Principles

The risk model for operations advocates these principles for successful risk management in operations:

- **Assess risks continuously.** This means the team never stops searching for new risks, and existing risks are periodically reevaluated.

- **Integrate risk management into every role and every function.** At a high level, this means that every IT role shares part of the responsibility for managing risk, and every IT process is designed with risk management in mind.

- **Treat risk identification positively.** For risk management to succeed, team members must be willing to identify risk without fear of retribution or criticism.

- **Use risk-based scheduling.** Maintaining an environment often means making changes in a sequence. Where possible the team should make the riskiest changes first to avoid wasting time and resources on changes that cannot be released.

- **Establish an acceptable level of formality.** Success requires a process that the team understands and uses.

These principles are summarized by the word *proactive*. A team that practices proactive risk management acknowledges that risk is a normal part of operations, and instead of fearing it, the team views it as an opportunity to safeguard the future. Team members demonstrate a proactive mindset by adopting a visible, measurable, repeatable, continuous process through which they objectively evaluate risks and opportunities and take action that addresses risks' causes as well as symptoms.

More MOF Information

The following Web sites contain more detailed information on MOF:

- *http://www.microsoft.com/technet/treeview/default.asp?url=/technet/ ittasks/plan/sysplan/mofovrv.asp*

- *http://www.microsoft.com/business/downloads/services/ mofdatasheet.doc*

- *http://www.microsoft.com/business/services/mcsmof.asp*

How the Frameworks Work Together

These frameworks support each other at different times and places. That is a key point to take from this chapter. Each of the three methodologies is targeted at different phases of the technology life cycle, as shown in Figure 8-5. MRF is the upstream planning function. MSF occurs at midpoint, and although it includes planning matters, it is really oriented toward the development and deployment activities. MOF is the downstream operations function for functions such as ongoing system maintenance.

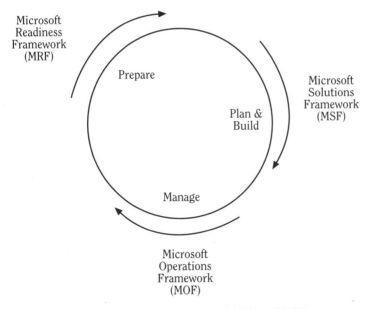

Figure 8-5.   *Bringing it all together: MRF, MSF, and MOF.*

MRF helps IT organizations develop individual and organizational readiness to use Microsoft's products and technologies. This guidance includes assessment and readiness-planning tools, learning roadmaps, readiness-related white papers, self-paced training, courses, certification exams, and readiness events.

MSF focuses on the planning, building, and deployment of various types of solutions. These solutions may be a line-of-business (LOB) application, an e-commerce Web site, an infrastructure project, a messaging solution, and so on. MSF provides guidance in the form of white papers, deployment guides, accelerated solutions, solution kits, case studies, and courseware in the areas of enterprise architecture, application development, component design, and infrastructure deployment.

MOF addresses the operations aspects of these solutions and helps IT organizations run mission-critical production systems based on Microsoft technologies by focusing on reliability, availability, and manageability. MOF includes a comprehensive suite of operational guidance in the form of white papers, operations guides, assessment tools, operations kits, best practices, case studies, and support tools that address the people, processes, and technologies for effectively managing systems within today's complex distributed IT environment.

So how do these models relate to Microsoft Solution for Internet Business? First, the prescriptive architectural guidance (PAG) component of the Microsoft Solution for Internet Business (to be defined in *Chapter 10, "Microsoft Solution for Internet Business and the Future"*), incorporates many of the specific features of the MRF, MSF, and MOF. Second, in business and technology, models are presented to provide a starting point. Often, individuals select the parts of a model that work well for them and ignore less germane components. This is expected to occur as you relate the MRF, MSF, and MOF to Microsoft Solution for Internet Business.

Common Framework Scenario

Within an organization, when a change requirement is identified, it will come from either the organization's strategic business planning process or within the IT operation itself. If it is triggered from the strategic planning process, MRF enables the organization to define the capabilities and risks associated with the new strategic direction. If it comes from within the IT operation, it is triggered through the change-management process if the organization is following the MOF practice. A review of this change incident would typically trigger an MRF project to assess the impact of the change on the business process, organizational capability requirements, or individuals. It might also trigger an MSF project to develop or deploy some new technology to address it. The contact points from each project team would be the content logistics management role from MRF, the logistics management role from MSF, and the release and configuration management role from MOF. This virtual team would represent the needs of the other two project teams to determine hand-offs and dependencies among teams. The program management of each project team would also work together to identify project dependencies and check in on critical milestones. The representative from the business would ideally play the role of product management to all three teams to ensure that the needs of the business are being appropriately addressed.

Organization

For MRF to help an organization prepare for a solution, the MRF team must identify the gap between the organization's current readiness state and the state it needs to be in to successfully plan, build, and operate the solution. To identify this gap, MRF relies on information from MSF and MOF about the requirements of the process or project and the participating roles. MRF can then establish the capabilities and priority levels required and assess whether these required processes or technologies are currently in use within the cus-tomer's organization. MRF next identifies the gap between the MSF and MOF requirements and the current state of the organization, and it benchmarks the organization and its individuals in an assessment.

Individual

At the individual level, MRF works with MSF and MOF to prepare the people within an organization to succeed with the solution. MSF and MOF first iden-tify the roles and describe the processes needed to make a project or process successful. MRF then helps the organization get ready for those processes and projects by identifying the competencies required of those individuals and describing the level of proficiency for those desired competencies. MRF next provides a learning plan for individuals to get them to the level required to successfully participate in the process or project described by the MSF or MOF plan.

Summary

This chapter was about methodologies in the context of Microsoft frameworks. MRF, MSF, and MOF were defined, and you were shown how these models interact and work together as a complete methodology. In the context of

Internet solutions, specifically Microsoft Solution for Internet Business, the emphasis was placed on the MSF and its development and deployment view, but the operations-related MOF is applicable to Microsoft Solution for Internet Business as well. For more information on these frameworks, visit *http://www.microsoft.com/solutions* (in addition to specific references cited in this chapter).

In the next chapter, project management topics are presented to help you successfully manage your Internet solutions project.

Technical Deployment Overview

The book now takes a marked shift to the technical side of Internet solutions. In the next chapter, the nuts and bolts of project management are presented, followed by technical specifics about the Microsoft Solution for Internet Business. This part of the book then concludes with a forward-looking view focused on the electronic commerce sector and enhancements to Microsoft Solution for Internet Business.

Project Management

Some things never change. What worked in the industrial era of J.P. Morgan—balancing time, cost, and performance considerations—works equally well in the Internet solutions era. That is, the fundamentals of project management are largely the same even though the ways in which such skills are applied have changed. In the past, project management was most often applied in construction, whereas today project management is being used for technology implementation projects. Looking at the project management fundamentals in Figure 9-1, you can see that a technology manager must skillfully balance time, cost, and performance levels all in the context of efficiently allocating resources and maintaining good relations with project stakeholders.

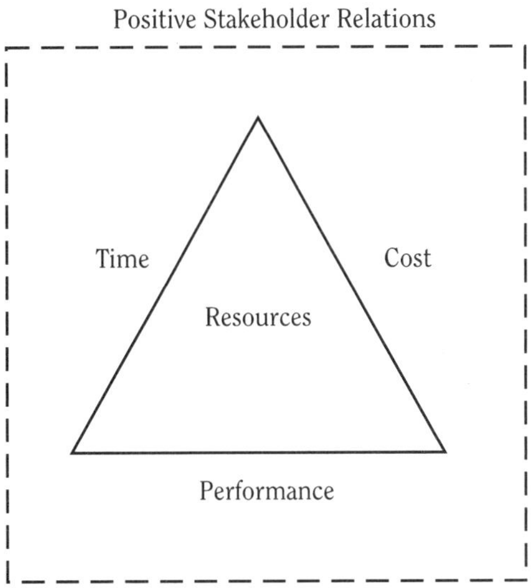

Figure 9-1. *Project management model.*

Each element of the project management model is challenging, to say the least, in the Internet era. Just ask the online legal services firm VersusLaw (see *Chapter 2, "Real-World Business Problems Seeking Solutions"*), which is surprisingly profitable, having grown slowly from modest roots as a modem-based bulletin board system (BBS) nearly 20 years ago. When the firm converted to an Internet platform using state-of-the-art Microsoft solutions, it quickly learned that its early schedule milestones and deadlines were overly optimistic. Likewise, although it estimated its hard costs with a great deal of accuracy for hardware and software, other costs were more difficult to accurately determine. First and foremost were difficulties in budgeting for billable consulting hours charged for this Internet implementation project. Additionally, the firm's experience in trying to accurately account for internal staff time associated with the project should not be minimized. More internal staff time than anticipated was used on the project. In short, it was more difficult than it first appeared. Although Versus-Law was satisfied with the technology outcome, an observation not lost on the participants was that they dodged problem areas that bedevil many technology-related projects, including successful completion. In many cases, technology projects don't enjoy a positive outcome because the technology solution is over-sold or poorly implemented.

In reality, "traditional" projects in construction and other businesses have more successful outcomes than technology-based projects. Why? Because the project management track record, and thus the accumulated knowledge base, is greater for these traditional projects. If you believe in learning from your experiences, you could say project management capabilities in the construction field (dating back to the Egyptian pyramids) are well learned and perhaps more refined than the Johnny-come-lately technology sector (relatively speaking when viewed over thousands of years). Because Internet solution projects are relatively new, the project management curve is steeper, the success scorecard shorter, and the knowledge base smaller. This is an accepted fact in the business community seeking to migrate core operations to the Internet.

So what are the lessons learned when applying the traditional project management model to Internet solutions? Leading the list would be expectation management. Project management in the Internet solution realm is even more treacherous than other technology projects based on well-established solutions. Your expectations should be adjusted accordingly, starting low and cautiously trusting the project management process as you see results. In no case should your expectations be set at the "assured outcome" level with Internet solutions. They are much more complex than other technologies, and anticipating an assured outcome would be foolhardy. In this chapter, we'll take a close look at the management side of project management with a definition of project team roles and responsibilities and even a description of project management certifications that can be earned. We will also look at the specific job duties of the project manager. This is followed by technical sections on project management, including the statement of work, specifications, work breakdown structure, and scheduling. The chapter concludes with discussion of the different project phases.

Roles and Responsibilities

This section imparts critical knowledge about the different stakeholders intimately involved in a project. This includes a project manager job description, training and certification considerations, and different forms of consulting support.

Job Description

In the quest to successfully staff a project management organization, several questions are typically asked on the front end of the staffing process, including:

- What is required for the person to become a successful project manager?
- What team members should make up the project team?
- What particular challenges are there in staffing a project team?
- What downstream events might result in the departure of a project team member?

Although simplistic on the surface, these questions take on a new, complex meaning when you consider that your project manager might be working on more than one project simultaneously. That is, the project manager and other project team members might not be dedicated strictly to your Internet solutions project.

Each project is different, and that is one of the unique staffing requirements when building a project team. A project team that is successful under one set of circumstances might not be successful on another project. This holds true more in the technology area than in other fields because any two technology projects can be radically different and thus have limited repetition and accumulated knowledge transfer. There are, however, "fundamentals" that a successful project manager must have irrespective of the specific engagement:

- **Stakeholder liaison.** The project manager must be able to successfully communicate with internal and external clients. This includes business decision makers (BDMs).
- **Project direction.** The project manager and the project team must be able to provide scope and vision for the project.

- **Project planning.** Strategic and tactical planning capabilities are essential. Remember that strategy is a broader concept than tactics and tactics are how strategies are implemented.

- **Project control.** More often than not, project management success is attributable to management know-how, such as the ability to control time and financial expenditures on a project. The ability to create a project schedule and budget is essential.

- **Project evaluation.** Conducting evaluations at certain points of the project, followed by an extensive project audit at the end, allows for complete accountability and reflection.

- **Project reporting.** Often, more than specific milestones being reached and budgets being met, projects can be measured by the amount of communications among the project manager, project team, and stakeholders. The communication can take several forms, the most familiar of which is the project schedule.

All of the other attributes that make a successful business person are prerequisites for a project manager, including understanding of personnel problems, technological knowledge, business management competence, versatility, and decision-making ability.

As alluded to earlier, the nature of a technology project, such as the implementation of an Internet solution, can vary widely from project to project. Consequently, it's not unusual for BDMs and human resources managers to struggle in determining what a project manager job description should contain.

The following is a specific project manager job description for an Internet solutions project.

Internet Solution Project Manager Duties
Under minimal supervision, the project manager establishes priorities and directs the efforts of personnel, including consultants and contractors, to be involved in the Internet solution project. This includes those individuals working on specific project tasks designed to achieve and fulfill an integrated set of technical, staffing, cost, and schedule requirements related to the Internet solution. Specifically, the project manager:

- Directs the development of initial and revised detailed task descriptions and forecasts their associated technical, staffing, cost, and schedule requirements for tasks assigned to the Information Technology (IT) department on the project.

- Directs the regular integration of initial and revised task forecasts into technical, staffing, cost, and schedule reports. Initiates the project-related approval cycle (including BDM approval) for the reports.

- Reviews conflicting functional business department, IT department, and project task recommendations or actions that occur from the initial task description and forecasts until final task completion. Directs uniform methods for conflict resolution.

- Evaluates available and planned additions to the project's staffing resources, including task applications for those resources, against integrated technical and staffing reports. Initiates actions to assure project staffing resource needs are met by the most economical mixture of available qualified consultants and contractors.

- Evaluates project cost and schedule reports in light of new tasks and changes in existing tasks. Initiates actions to ensure that increases and decreases in task costs and project schedules are acceptable and approved by key stakeholders, including BDMs.

- Prioritizes, adjusts, and directs the efforts of project personnel (including consultants and contractors) resource allocations as necessary to ensure adherence to integrated staffing, cost, and project schedule commitments.

- Regularly reports the results of project staffing, cost, and schedule evaluations to BDMs.

- Regularly directs the development of individual tasks with project personnel, including individual task descriptions and associated resource and duration forecasts.

- Directs creation and issuance of integrated project progress reports.

- Recommends new project strategies, goals, and objectives in light of anticipated long-term staffing and budget needs.

- Establishes basic organizational and personnel qualification requirements for performance on tasks, including those by consultants and contractors.

- Establishes the requirements for, directs the development of, and approves control programs to standardize methods used for controlling similar types of activities on this project and future similar projects.

- Establishes the requirements for, directs the development of, and approves training as necessary for project personnel.

- Approves recommendations for the procurement of materials and services as evidenced by purchase orders and ensures that these purchases are consistent with approved cost and schedule reports.

- Promotes harmonious relations among project personnel and other stakeholders (including BDMs) involved with the project.

- Completes other duties as related to the project.

Qualifications

- A bachelor of science degree in engineering or computer science, or a business degree with a minor in engineering or computer science. Professional designation (CompTIA Project+ and Microsoft Certified Professional [MCP] preferred, with extra consideration given to Microsoft Certified System Engineer[MCSE]/Microsoft Certified Solution Developer [MCSD]/Microsoft Certified Database Administrator [MCDBA])

- Five or more years of management experience including a minimum of two years of supervisory experience in a technology-related field and two years of technology project management experience.

- Working knowledge of Internet solution design and implementation issues such as operation system installation, application development, and network infrastructure matters.

- Demonstrated capability to develop high-level management control programs.

- Experience related to computer-based cost and scheduling applications.

Finally, don't use the project management role for an "up or out" management philosophy. As you may know, in the military, the phrase *up or out* addresses the need for receiving continual promotions or being nudged into retirement to make room for others. Individuals should not be promoted to the project manager role simply because they are due for a promotion or they are at the top of their pay grade. Being named a project manager should be based on merit and be considered an honor and a privilege, nothing less.

Performance Measures

Professionals, such as project managers, have come to expect regular merit pay increases, typically for a job well done. This expectation includes increases even when performance is below grade under the guise of "inflationary" increases. Adding to the compensation mix, it is difficult to credit or blame a single individual with project success or failure. All of these factors combine to make the human resources management area difficult and challenging. Here is a sample set of performance measures for project managers on an Internet solutions project:

- Success in directing agreed-on tasks toward completion:
  - Technical implementation according to requirements
  - Quality
  - Key milestones and schedules
  - Target costs, design-to-cost
  - Innovation
  - Trade-offs

- Effectiveness as a team member or team leader:
  - Building an effective task team
  - Working with others, participation, involvement
  - Communicating with support organizations and subcontractors
  - Interfunctional coordination (coordination between functional departments)
  - Getting along with others
  - Changing orientation
  - Making and fulfilling commitments

- Success and effectiveness in performing functional tasks in addition to project work in accordance with functional charter:
  - Special assignments
  - Advancing technology
  - Developing organization
  - Resource planning
  - Functional direction and leadership

- Administrative support services:
  - Reports and reviews
  - Special task forces and committees
  - Project planning
  - Procedure development

- New business development:
  - Additional work
  - Bid proposal support
  - Customer presentations

- Professional development:
  - Keeping abreast in professional field
  - Publications
  - Liaison with Microsoft certification community, vendors, customers, and education institutions

- Additional considerations:
  - Difficulty of tasks involved: technical challenges, state-of-the-art considerations, changes, and contingencies
  - Managerial responsibilities: task leader for project personnel, multifunctional integration, budget responsibility, staffing responsibility, specific accountabilities
  - Multiproject involvement: number of different projects, number and magnitude of functional tasks and duties, overall workload.

Training and Certification

The types of individuals in project management on an Internet solutions project often are very different from what you might imagine. Whereas the technical participants are likely to have degrees in computer science or electrical engineering, a project manager is more likely to have a business degree, perhaps even a Master of Business Administration (MBA). Having Microsoft technical certifications such as MCSD and MCSE are germane to the efforts of the technical team, but the project management team will likely have different certifications.

One such certification to be considered by the project manager and others is the IT Project+ designation from CompTIA, a certification group. The cornerstone of IT Project+ is to assess skills and certify project management professionals based on three testing areas: business knowledge, interpersonal skills, and project management processes. Specifically, the exams measure the areas listed in Table 9-1.

Table 9-1.   CompTIA IT Project+ Exam Topics

Testing Area	Percentage of Examination
Scope definition	27%
Preliminary planning/project planning	39%
Project execution	29%
Closure	5%
Total	100%

Training for this type of project management certification occurs at private training centers that specifically prepare students to take the exam. This project management designation was acquired by CompTIA from Gartner Group. More information is available at *http://www.comptia.com.*

Alternatively, many business schools at both the undergraduate and graduate level offer project management degrees. Colleges offering MBAs with project management concentrations include the University of Denver and the University of Washington, among many others. Such a path should be considered for a senior-level project manager or a project management consultant seeking further professional development.

Consulting Support

Firms seeking to implement an Internet solution often realize that outside expertise trumps in-house capabilities with respect to project management. You can engage project management assistance from a number of capable service providers. Your technical consultant, typically a Microsoft Certified Partner, also might have capable project management resources on staff. This falls under the classic definition of utilizing an all-in-one service provider to implement your Internet solution but variations exist. For example, on the low end you might engage a sole practitioner who was previously employed by a large project management consulting firm. This can be an ideal relationship that results in lower fees. On the high end, the Big Five accounting firms and worldwide project management firms such as Bechtel are resources to consider in filling the project management role. Such firms charge accordingly (that is, commensurate with their size) and are acceptable selections when cost savings from the project management function is not an overriding concern. Most client firms select middle ground, weighing capabilities, costs, and prestige when selecting a project management consulting firm.

One Microsoft business unit that provides project management assistance, on a fee basis, is Microsoft Technology Centers (MTCs). Located in several parts of the United States, MTCs provide planning and project management assistance for Internet solutions projects in addition to a technical test lab. MTCs are discussed further in the Appendix.

Baseline Infrastructure

Prior to launch, several baseline tasks in an Internet solutions project need to be completed. These include tasks unique to Internet solutions projects such as:

- **Domain name registration.** Has your organization registered its domain names with the appropriate Internet registration authorities?

- **Service mark/trademark registration.** Have all business names and other identifying statements been properly registered to protect both your interests and investments in this area?

- **Legal miscellany.** Have you given proper consideration to the scope of project work as defined in a contract? Equally important, what contract administration procedures will you use during the course of the project? Are there any interstate or international commerce issues such as taxes, permits, export controls, or regulations?

Central to these points is the fact that any baseline infrastructure "showstoppers" must be addressed well before a project manager is engaged and an Internet solutions project commences. An example of a showstopper would be an outstanding applicable litigation that negatively affects the project.

The Project

At the heart of project management is the project itself. A *project* is easily defined as a collection of tasks, each with assigned durations, that form a project with a definitive start, interim milestones, and a finish. The key point is that a project is not an ongoing concern and it has a discrete end. Central to the project itself is the project schedule, which reflects information from a wide range of planning and operational documents such as the statement of work (SOW), specifications, work breakdown structure (WBS), and budgets.

Statement of Work

The SOW is a narrative description of the work required for the project. The complexity of the SOW is a function of both the desires of management (such as the BDMs) and the nature of the project itself. An Internet solutions project will likely have a more complex SOW than building a deck on a house. Typically, the SOW is prepared by internal staff with input from all of the stakeholders. However, outside consultants or contractors are sometimes retained to assist in SOW creation. Be advised that one common mistake is to have a very technical person write the SOW. Instead, an individual with general skills (such as business skills) should be the writer so that the SOW isn't laden with scientific terminology that is difficult to read. In fact, the BDM might be the best person to write the SOW. After preparation, the SOW is submitted to the stakeholders for verification and approval.

Although the following is a finer point of project management, it is nonetheless a point well taken. In competitive bidding environments, there are often two SOWs: the proposal SOW and the contractual SOW.

Proposal SOW

The proposal SOW is part of the request for proposal (RFP) document and process. The proposal SOW allows an "apples-to-apples" bidding situation that is ethical and fair for the contractors, vendors, and consultants bidding on the work. The proposal SOW is often based on incomplete information and as such will be modified and otherwise enhanced by the incumbent contractors, vendors, and consultants.

Contractual SOW

The contractual SOW is typically created after the selection of the project contractors, vendors, and consultants. Based on a more complete understanding of the Internet solutions project, the contractual SOW is typically more detailed and authoritative. Extra care must be exercised to reconcile the differences between the proposal SOW and the contractual SOW. Such differences are acceptable because the proposal SOW is intended to be a preliminary description that was uniform for all competitive bidders. However, once the project contracts are negotiated and prepared for signing, the contractual SOW prevails over the proposal SOW.

To put it another way, a winning proposal is no guarantee that any of the parties understands the SOW. However, the contractual SOW assumes that all parties understand the work to be accomplished. For large projects, there is often a fact-finding step to uncover and mediate any misunderstandings. This allows all parties to agree on the contractual SOW with the following understandings:

- What work is required
- What work is proposed
- The factual basis for the costs
- Other related matters

SOW Preparation

SOW preparation isn't as easy as it first appears. Misinterpretation of the SOW can result in delays, lower quality, and cost overruns. Consider the following Internet solutions situations:

- You are the incumbent outside consultant on a large Internet solution project. The contractual SOW calls for a minimum of two beta cycles on the solution before it is to be considered ready for real-world use. To be safe, you plan for three beta cycles. However, at the end of the third beta cycle, the client reports that the results are substandard (too many bugs) and there are lingering performance issues. You, the outside consultant, conduct another beta round to resolve the client's concerns. This is at significant expense to you and isn't compensated by the client.

- The SOW states that the outside consultant must test the Internet solution with a live Internet connection. The client's expectation was for a connection at the same speed that would be used in the actual deployment. To cut corners and save money, the outside consultant tests the Internet solution over a simple broadband connection from a home, such as Digital Subscriber Line (DSL). Thus, the final Internet solution isn't optimized for a faster connection, resulting in a lower level of quality than the client anticipated.

As these two scenarios point out, SOW misinterpretation can occur. Common causes for these misinterpretations include:

- Project management concepts such as tasks, milestones, specifications, and special instructions, being mixed together

- Use of unclear, vague, and imprecise language

- Poorly structured writing with no pattern or chronological order

- Inconsistent sizing of tasks (ideally all tasks should be similar in size; larger tasks can be broken down and smaller tasks can be consolidated to achieve this)

- Different writers describing the work differently in the same SOW (a function of poor editing on the back end of the SOW creation process)

- Third-party and stakeholder review step skipped to save time

Here is another important point about an SOW: it is truly a statement and not a fully detailed specification of the work. Ideally, the SOW is no longer than two pages. The following checklist is a guide for writers and editors in creating the SOW:

- Clear task descriptions are essential. The writer must understand that stakeholders from many walks of life (technical, business, legal, and so on) will likely be reading the SOW. A good SOW states precisely the product or service desired to avoid ambiguity.

- Passages that take control of the work away from the contractor, vendor, or consultant also relieve the same party of responsibility. Use procedures if necessary to enhance control ("will seek client's approval").

- Use active, not passive, terminology and limit abbreviations to those in common usage.

- Make certain that the SOW is specific enough to allow the contractor, vendor, or consultant to make sound decisions about the staffing and other resources needed to accomplish each element.

- The specific duties of the contractor, vendor, or consultant should be enumerated so that the parties to the project can assess compliance.

- When attempting to maintain brevity in the SOW, it is permissible to reference outside documents, but double-check that the references are correct.

- Directions should be clearly separated from general comments.

- All organizational contracting and procurement processes must be followed in creating the SOW. Make sure the SOW isn't at odds with normal business practices at the client firm.

- Security requirements should be adequately addressed. This could include the nondisclosure nature of the project as evidenced by a nondisclosure agreement (NDA). In an Internet solutions project, it might include statements about computer and network security.

Specifications

Next in the project process are the specifications. Specifications are widely used in the software development process and Internet solutions are no exception. *Specifications* are standards for pricing out a proposal. They are typically very detailed and can include screen shots, performance benchmarks, user interface (UI) examples, and the like.

It is important to understand the critical role that specifications play in a project. If and when litigation related to a project occurs, courts have typically found that the project specifications take precedence over anything else, including drawings or prototypes. If it exists in the specifications, a feature or function is considered to be "official." Contrast that with a drawing on a whiteboard, which won't trump the project specifications in court.

Creating the specifications is the same as *scoping,* a term typically used in technology projects when an individual creates the scope of work.

Work Breakdown Structure

The WBS is a critical document in the project management process that is often overlooked. At the highest level, affectionately referred to by business executives as the 50,000-foot level, the WBS is the document that drives the project scheduling function. That order of precedence is important to understand. Dropping lower, to the 10,000-foot level of understanding, the WBS can be thought of as an extremely detailed list of tasks that are further broken down into subtasks and sub-subtasks. In other words, tasks are broken down to the lowest level of minute detail. The WBS structure is shown in Table 9-2. Note that the top three levels of the WBS are typically specified by the client and the lower levels are generated by the contractors, vendors, and consultants that actually perform the work.

Table 9-2.   Work Breakdown Structure

Level	Label	Description
1	1.0	Total Program
2	1.1	Project
3	1.1.1	Task
4	1.1.1.1	Subtask
5	1.1.1.1.1	Work Package
6	1.1.1.1.1.1	Level of Effort

Let's discuss the WBS between these two viewpoints or the middle ground. In planning a project, the project manager structures the work into small elements that are manageable, integratable, and measurable. *Manageable* refers to the ability to assign specific authority and responsibility. An example would be assigning a specific developer to create a specific set of SQL stored procedures. *Integratable* refers to having all detailed tasks lead up to a completed project. That is, by viewing the WBS and "walking the ladder" of tasks you should be able to see the whole picture. WBS elements must also be *measurable* in terms of progress. That is, the completion of a WBS task must indicate project progress, not digression.

Like the SOW, there can be two WBS documents: the one used in the proposal phase and the one used in the project phase. This might occur for the same reasons there are often two SOWs, including a uniform bidding process and a more detailed follow-up WBS after the winning contractors, vendors, and consultants have been selected.

Harold Kerzner, in his book *Project Management: A Systems Approach to Planning, Scheduling and Controlling* (John Wiley & Sons, 2001), observed that "WBS is the single most important element because it provides a common framework from which:

- The total program can be cited as a summation of subdivided elements.
- Planning can be performed.
- Costs and budgets can be established.
- Time, cost, and performance can be tracked.
- Objectives can be linked to company resources in a logical manner.
- Schedules and status-reporting procedures can be established.
- Network construction and control planning can be initiated.
- The responsibility assignments for each element can be established."

Budgets

Central to the financial success of a project is the budgeting process. Budgets not only are used as a management tool, but they also directly affect the ROI of an Internet solutions project (this concept is discussed in both *Chapter 5, "Creating Business Value,"* and *Chapter 6, "Benefits Analysis: Creating a Base Dynamic Internet Presence"*). At the most basic level, project budgeting is nothing more than estimating the costs associated with the project. It often occurs using a spreadsheet program such as Microsoft Excel. Columns contain time periods and rows contain dates. This is a process familiar to most BDMs.

What might be more perplexing is the act of creating accurate budgets for a technology project such as implementing an Internet solution. Often, costs are difficult to estimate or they change over time in unexpected ways. This is normal and can best be accommodated by creating frequent revised project budgets. For example, hardware costs tend to decline over time and labor costs often increase.

Revised project budgets can help you avoid surprises and they are part of the overall expectation management process in an Internet solutions project. Budget adjustments (either increases or decreases) are fine as long as the accounting stays on target (budgets stay current) and the stakeholders are regularly updated on budgeting matters.

Different budgeting techniques include guesstimation, extrapolation, and zero-based budgeting.

Guesstimation

Pragmatically speaking, budgets are often crafted in the real world using the "on-the-fly" approach of guessing. BDMs, comfortable that they have a reasonable idea of what the costs will be and with little time to engage in other budgeting approaches, simply input cost guesses in a spreadsheet. Unfortunately, this approach is used much more than the authors (and we suspect the readers) of this book would like to admit.

The guessing game works better for construction than for technology projects. Why? Because in construction, you have common cost denominators such as cost per square foot. An individual could simply look at the size of a building and quickly guess at the costs. No such common cost denominators exist for technology projects because of the uniqueness of each one.

Extrapolation

The extrapolation budgeting approach works well on traditional projects. For example, take a 40,000-square-foot Class A office building that was recently completed. The project manager or individual responsible for project budgeting can likely take the budget used on the aforementioned project and apply it to another construction project of similar size and scope. This is a common practice and the "new" budget for the forthcoming office building is adjusted slightly for local conditions, such as changes in materials prices and the like.

Zero-Based Budgeting

Although the zero-based budgeting approach is certainly the most painstaking, it is also the most accurate. Here, an individual with project budgeting responsibilities accurately assesses each cost component. This is typically accomplished by calling all involved parties and obtaining detailed cost bids. For example, if a temporary WAN is to be implemented during the Internet solutions project, the person responsible for budgeting would call the telecommunications provider for data transmission cost bids and a hardware supplier for router and channel service unit/data service unit (CSU/DSU) bid information.

Zero-based budgeting requires a significant expenditure of time, but many BDMs feel that the resulting more accurate project is well worth the extra effort. Note that competent project scheduling applications such as Microsoft Project can accommodate budgeting information in addition to the requisite time and resources entries.

Planning

First things first: a project starts with upfront planning. Typically, the work specifications are generated first, followed by the WBS, a basic task outline that is used to generate the project schedule. A project schedule can be displayed in several ways, including a Gantt chart and a PERT/CPM chart.

A Gantt chart is a simple timeline followed from left to right showing project tasks. It is one of the easiest project schedules to understand and is typically most appropriate for a business audience. However, for a more accurate and detailed project schedule perspective, consider the Program Evaluation Review Technique/Critical Path Method (PERT/CPM) chart. This type of chart, shown in Figure 9-2, shows the critical path, which by definition is the line between tasks that have no slack time. Restated, if a task on the critical path is delayed, the entire project suffers a delay. A delayed task on the non-critical path does not necessarily delay the entire project.

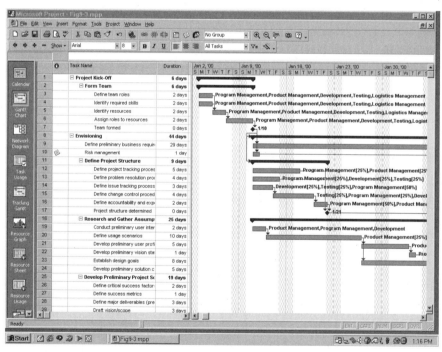

Figure 9-2.   *Gantt chart for an Internet solutions project.*

Another interesting piece of information from PERT/CPM charts is how predecessor and successor relationships are displayed. A Gantt chart suggests that tasks across a linear timeline have an implicit predecessor/successor relationship, but this is often not the case in the real world. Worse yet, a task on the first page of a Gantt chart may actually have a predecessor/successor relationship with a task on the third or fourth page. This would not be apparent.

A PERT/CPM chart displays predecessor/successor relationships with connecting lines. However, a PERT/CPM chart does not accurately display task durations or time. Therefore, you need both Gantt and PERT/CPM charts to accurately plan your Internet solutions project. A PERT/CPM chart is displayed in Figure 9-3.

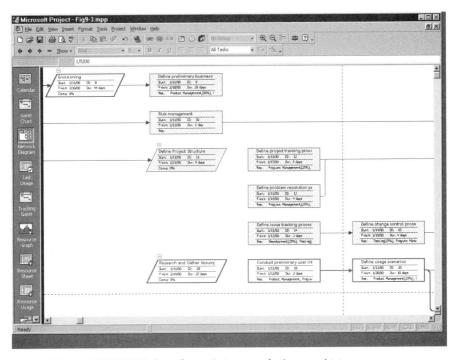

Figure 9-3. *A PERT/CPM chart for an Internet solutions project.*

Project Work

The planning activities set the stage for the actual commencement of the project work in which the developers and system engineers craft your Internet solution. Project schedules are an often overlooked element of the project work phase. Rather than allowing the project schedules to be used only for planning purposes and then languish, these reports should be constantly updated during the entire life of the project. This allows the schedules to reflect delta or incremental changes to the original plan. Sophisticated project management applications, such as Microsoft Project 2002, facilitate schedule updating by allowing you to define your original work as the baseline schedule.

Deployment

After building and testing an Internet solution, you are ready to deploy it for actual use. It might make more sense to view the deployment as a second project separate from the planning and creating of the Internet solution because deployment has a distinctly different mind-set associated with solution development. It is also likely that, as you've developed the Internet solution, you have very different ideas about how the Internet solution should be deployed (versus what your original deployment thoughts were).

Support

Considered a downstream operations function, the support role is initially under the jurisdiction of the project team. Support includes two specific functions. The first function is the support activities for maintaining the Internet solution itself. The second function is the support activities for customers, which can take a variety of traditional forms, ranging from call centers to e-mail.

Once the project is complete (or nearly complete), the support activities are transferred back into the traditional functional organization. This is a common practice in project management.

Project Audit

An essential component to learning from successes and failures when deploying Internet solutions is a postproject audit. To ensure that the audit is legitimate and not a façade, consider using a separate team (perhaps outsiders such as an accounting firm) to critically assess time management, budget, and the quality of project deliverables. Project audits often pay for themselves directly by identifying overpayments to vendors and the like, and such audits effectively serve as the baseline for future Internet solution projects.

Project Team

Constructing the project team is very interesting to say the least. A project team can look dramatically different from firm to firm and project to project because projects, especially in the Internet solutions realm, tend to be unique. Internet solutions are often custom work, not replicated from other clients or past implementation attempts within the firm.

Aside from the traditional project manager, scheduler, and core project team members, assess the fitness of the following potential project team members for your Internet solutions project:

- **External stakeholders including end users and customers.** Consider an advisory panel, beta testers, and early adopters.

- **Technical.** Developers, quality assurance personnel, Web site designers, content providers, and customer support fall into this category.

- **Infrastructure.** These roles include IT/IS site managers and network and data security managers.

- **Internal stakeholders.** Stakeholders include cross-department or intrabusiness partners: back-end integration stakeholders, transactional systems partners, accounting, shipping and receiving, and so on.

- **Other.** Other team members can be added as dictated by the requirements of your specific project.

Summary

In reality, the use of bona fide project management techniques does not ensure successful Internet solutions. However, sans a project management mechanism, an Internet solution development and deployment is assuredly doomed to failure. The key point is to pragmatically apply the "best-of-breed" project management approaches, many of which were presented in this chapter. Because Internet solutions are more often than not custom work, it requires skill to find a workable balance between small (nimble, rapid development and deployment) and large (thorough planning and communication, intradepartmental buy-in) project management efforts. In the next chapters, the specific nature of Microsoft Solution for Internet Business is explored.

Microsoft Solution for Internet Business: The Solution Set

The message you should take away from this book is that, given the Internet solution planning topics presented throughout, you are closer than ever to being in a good position to pick an Internet solution. Obviously there are several ways to select an Internet solution. This chapter provides details of the Microsoft Solution for Internet Business , one of the solutions available to your organization. Now that the bulk of the book is behind you, you have a basic understanding of Internet solutions from the viewpoint of a business decision maker (BDM). Microsoft Solution for Internet Business is really a combination solution like few others offered by Microsoft. It comes in two versions: Microsoft Solution for Internet Business and Microsoft Solution for Internet Business–Retail Extension. The baseline version of Microsoft Solution for Internet Business is intended as the starting point for Web sites that do not actually offer products for sale. Microsoft Solution for Internet Business–Retail Extension is intended for Web sites through which products are actually sold. It has four primary components, which are the focus of the main sections of this chapter: software, prescriptive architectural guidance (PAG), services, and support. All of these combine to form the Microsoft Solution for Internet Business solution shown in Figure 10-1.

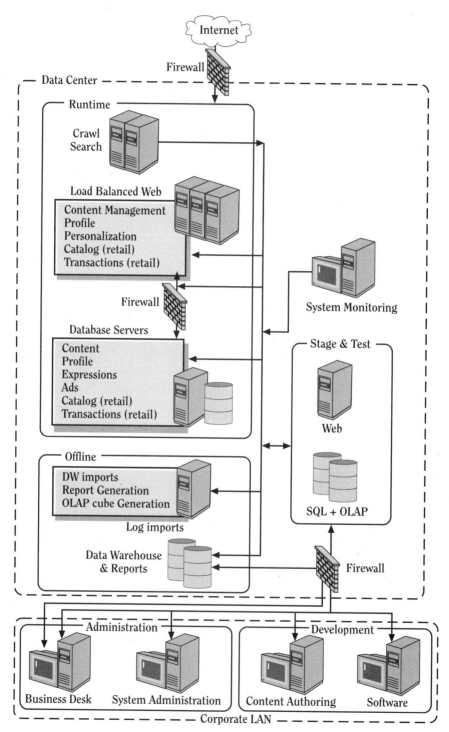

Figure 10-1. *The Microsoft Solution for Internet Business solution.*

All told, Microsoft Solution for Internet Business is a comprehensive solution that is clearly beyond the capabilities of individual applications such as Microsoft Commerce Server. The three Ss are software, services, and support, but the fourth S is solution. The software component includes the underlying Microsoft Windows 2000 Server operating system and Microsoft .NET Enterprise servers. The services component is comprised primarily of Microsoft Certified Partners (MCPs) such as consulting firms and Microsoft Consulting Services (MCS). These firms provide Microsoft Solution for Internet Business planning and deployment services. The third component, support, relates to various forms of support, including Microsoft Support Options (MSO). To this mix, add PAG, which is essentially a set of architectural reference documents. These all combine to create the "big S"—the solution known as Microsoft Solution for Internet Business, which includes additional benefits such as rapid deployment and ease of maintenance. Each of these component areas is discussed next, starting with the big picture: defining the solution first and then exploring each component in more detail.

Solution Introduction

Microsoft Solution for Internet Business is a complete Internet solution for medium and large businesses that want a structured deployment, ease of maintenance, and vendor support. Microsoft provides prescriptive guidance for presales engineering, solution development, and operations. The software side of the solution is based on the industry-leading Windows .NET Enterprise servers. Microsoft Consulting Services, along with certified global integration partners and Microsoft Gold Certified Partners, participate in the planning and deployment of the Microsoft Solution for Internet Business software for the customer. Support comes in the form of Microsoft support arrangements that meet the immediate needs of the enterprise. This takes the form of premier support with a single point of contact that provides additional incident hours and quicker response time guarantees (for example, one hour for emergencies). It also means the customer will receive technical support from engineers trained on the Microsoft Solution for Internet Business solution, not just the individual components.

This section looks at the Microsoft Solution for Internet Business life cycle and the benefits of using Microsoft Solution for Internet Business. Later in the chapter, after the next three S components of software, services, and support are presented, the "Solution Summary" section ties all of the components together.

Microsoft Solution for Internet Business Solution Life Cycle

There are four phases in the Microsoft Solution for Internet Business life cycle: presales engineering, planning and designing, implementation, and operations and management.

Presales Engineering

It's not lost on BDMs that key drivers in the Microsoft Solution for Internet Business purchase decision are cost and competitive considerations. Microsoft Solution for Internet Business deployment costs are reduced by having a structured implementation methodology, including PAG. The structured methodology and prescriptive guidance are based on a proven and tested configuration, which increases the chances that the solution will be implemented successfully. Note that Microsoft Solution for Internet Business was validated first in Microsoft labs and later in production by industry-leading companies around the world. Based on all this, the Microsoft Solution for Internet Business consultant can accurately estimate the size and cost of the solution that will fill your needs. Another presales engineering component is the use of accelerator sites for prototyping and building mock-ups and demos. This allows customers to see how the Microsoft Solution for Internet Business solution actually works in their situations and allows a business to determine that quick, competitive responses are possible. Here, a business can see that as business conditions change rapidly, the Microsoft Solution for Internet Business Web site can be modified and updated at the same speed.

Planning and Designing

In the planning and designing phases, several tasks occur, including detailing design creation, identifying users and stakeholders, building a security plan, and identifying postproduction support needs. Microsoft Solution for Internet Business supports these tasks in several ways. Microsoft Solution for Internet Business leverages existing architectures; that is, the different Microsoft Solution for Internet Business solutions for corporate, online retail, prototyping, and government can be easily modified to fit your needs. This form of leverage might include integrating with both existing Internet commerce applications and databases and an existing network backbone infrastructure. Microsoft Solution for Internet Business customers also benefit from learning curve analysis, where the repetition of Microsoft Solution for Internet Business deployments lowers costs by allowing the deployment team to engage in best practices and avoid missteps. You can thus tap into the wealth of existing Microsoft Solution for Internet Business knowledge that allows you to leverage up and effectively learn from others who have been there before. Included with that knowledge base is the predictability of development durations and site sizes, again based on the experience of others, including PAG and best practices. Further, the knowledge built up by the Microsoft Solution for Internet Business community of developers, partners, and customers also allows you to understand what downstream support issues await you. You can also manage your expectations with respect to future support needs, such as budgeting for support needs and future network cost outlays.

Implementation

As a general rule, sound technology planning and deployment methodologies result in implementation building blocks. This is analogous to goals and objectives in strategic management that result in tactics (a standard business school lecture). The building blocks of the implementation phase are development, testing, initial staging, and deployment. Microsoft Solution for Internet Business supports the implementation phase by doing the following:

- Providing an accelerator site that provides a solid foundation for a high-quality, highly scalable Web site.

- Demonstrating best practices by including extensive use of caching and class libraries for error handling and database access.

- Providing prescriptive guidance for development that explains how to "skin a site," or modify what the solution provides within the accelerator site and make it your own unique site.

Operations and Management

This phase includes the following building blocks:

- **Site deployment and launch.** Microsoft Solution for Internet Business provides prescriptive guidance that helps customers rapidly deploy Microsoft Solution for Internet Business sites by filling the gap between traditional product documentation and knowledge about how to deploy the solution. Deployment includes data center configuration, security architecture, and scalability and availability issues.

- **Site monitoring.** Standard monitoring tools from the .NET applications are used to monitor Microsoft Solution for Internet Business sites.

- **Management of site security.** Microsoft Solution for Internet Business guidance includes best practices in operating and securing a site (such as backup policies and firewall configurations).

- **Follow-up site releases.** Microsoft is committed to actively enhancing and extending the Microsoft Solution for Internet Business solution.

Microsoft Solution for Internet Business Benefits

One design goal of Microsoft Solution for Internet Business was to include content management, analytics, personalization, and e-commerce capabilities to satisfy a broad audience. More important, the underlying intent of Microsoft Solution for Internet Business is to provide an Internet site that can be easily updated by nontechnical contributors. This includes the following tasks:

- Updating site content

- Changing logos

- Adding background colors

- Securing or removing pages

- Managing the merchandising function

- Creating and deploying promotions

- Running analytics to understand customer behavior

Additionally, Microsoft Solution for Internet Business empowers business managers to take control of this function in their businesses by either performing these tasks directly or assigning updating functions to key employees.

The following Microsoft Solution for Internet Business benefits accrue to the business manager:

- Realization of new business opportunities

- Creation of more effective marketing strategies

- Positive user experience on the Web sites

- Improved customer and partner loyalty

Business users can realize these benefits of Microsoft Solution for Internet Business:

- Empowerment to manage their own content and catalogs
- Creation of more effective marketing campaigns
- Less reliance on the IT group
- Immediate updates to the Web

Technical managers can expect the following benefits from Microsoft Solution for Internet Business:

- Fast time to market
- Leveraged IT investments
- Streamlined operations
- Empowerment of business users
- Integration with a variety of back-end systems

Software

The Microsoft Solution for Internet Business software discussion can be divided into three parts: .NET Enterprise servers; general hardware requirements; and specific Microsoft Solution for Internet Business solutions for corporate, online retail, prototyping, and government.

.NET Enterprise Servers

Several Microsoft .NET Enterprise Server products are incorporated in Microsoft Solution for Internet Business. This provides the functionality and features needed to build a complete Internet solution.

Microsoft Windows 2000 Advanced Server

The underlying network operating system, Microsoft Windows 2000 Advanced Server, is responsible for providing basic network functions such as security, file and print sharing, and support for running applications. This is a given, but let's take a moment to review some of the Windows 2000 Advanced Server features:

- **Security.** In addition to a next-generation NTFS file system (version 5) that provides extensive local and network resource security, Windows 2000 Advanced Server also has network and Internet security based on the latest standards: 56-bit and 12-bit secure socket layer (SSL), IP Security (IPSec), Kerberos v5 authentication, Server Gated Cryptography, Digest Authentication, and Fortezza. The public key infrastructure (PKI) capability is supported by the Certificate Server service that issues X.509 certificates. The Encryption File System (EFS) locks down data locally on the hard disk by encrypting it.

- **Web and Application Support.** This is a major area of functionality and support in Windows 2000 Advanced Server. This includes Internet Information Services 5.0 (IIS), which is an integrated Web service that enables the hosting and management of Web sites. IIS is also integrated with core operating systems and applications (such as Microsoft Exchange 2000 Server). A robust Active Server Pages (ASP) programming environment is supported, as is an XML parser. There is native support for Windows DNA (the Windows Distributed Network Architecture) and the Component Object Model+ (COM+).

- **Services.** Windows 2000 Advanced Server also provides a range of operating system–level services that support network and Internet connectivity, such as Dynamic Domain Name System (DNS) for name resolution, Windows Internet Name Service (WINS) for legacy name resolution, and Dynamic Host Configuration Protocol (DHCP) for Internet Protocol (IP) address assignment. The Routing and Remote Access service connects remote users and supports virtual private networks (VPNs). The VPN function in Windows 2000 Advanced Server is a full-featured gateway that encrypts communications to securely connect remote users and branch offices over the Internet using Point-to-Point Tunneling Protocol (PPTP) or the advanced security of Layer 2 Tunneling Protocol (L2TP) encrypted by IPSec.

- **Active Directory service.** This is the directory services component in Windows 2000 Advanced Server that provides a scalable networking infrastructure architecture for even the largest enterprises. Active Directory service manages the objects on a network such as users, computers, printers, domains, and the trust relationships among those domains. This is a core component of Windows 2000 Advanced Server.

- **Terminal Services.** This is a remote control capability that runs in two modes. At the most basic level, it is configured to run in Remote Administration mode, allowing two users to log on simultaneously. Typically one user logs on as the administrator and performs maintenance work such as downloading and applying a service pack (no additional licenses are needed). Terminal Services can also be configured in Application Sharing mode, which allows numerous users to log on simultaneously and run applications, for example, to work from home or while on the road. Note that Application Sharing mode requires additional Terminal Services client access licenses and places a significant load on the server machine (consumes RAM, takes foreground processor priority, and so on). However, in the context of Microsoft Solution for Internet Business, Terminal Services as a management tool allows someone to easily update a Web site from anywhere at any time. This includes performing Microsoft Solution for Internet Business system administration tasks or operations management.

- **Group Policy.** This is an Active Directory management tool that allows the administrator to richly configure the Windows 2000–based networking environment. Such configurations include desktop appearance and functionality, security template implementation, and software distribution.

Specific to the Advanced Server release of the Windows 2000 Server family, there is support for clustering, more processors (eight-way symmetric multiprocessor support), and large-scale RAM (support for 8 GB of RAM). Windows 2000 Server–related clustering is quickly configured with the Cluster Service Setup Wizard. It supports rolling upgrades to cluster members, avoiding downtime in critical Internet commerce environments. Furthermore, the clustering capability supports load balancing to allow your Web site to run more efficiently, as one server doesn't become overtaxed while others are underutilized). In addition to the increased uptime, two-node cluster service failover is supported, so a hardware failure does not disable your Web site.

Microsoft SQL Server (Enterprise Edition)

Microsoft SQL Server is Microsoft's entry in the powerful SQL database arena. This component acts as the database engine and storage facility for the Microsoft Solution for Internet Business solution. Note that Microsoft Solution for Internet Business requires the Enterprise Edition of SQL Server. A key point is the native integration of SQL Server with other .NET components such as Commerce Server and Microsoft BizTalk Server. SQL Server features the following capabilities:

- **Web-enabled.** SQL Server supports extensive database programming capabilities that conform to Web standards. This includes rich Hypertext Transfer Protocol (HTTP) and XML support, along with stored procedures that store and retrieve data in the XML format. The Web-enabled Analysis Services allows you to perform analytics on data across the Internet using a Web browser.

- **High scalability and reliability.** SQL Server takes advantage of multiprocessor support, scaling across servers, and clustering. Security is enforced natively and by Active Directory service.

- **Rapid development.** SQL Server features rapid development tools such as Analysis Services, Transact-SQL, preconfigured stored procedures, and support for Microsoft Visual Studio–based tools. Another example is Data Transformation Services (DTS), which uses automated routines that extract, transform, and parse data from several different sources.

- **Management.** SQL Server is managed from easy-to-master native tools such as the Enterprise Manager and a plethora of wizards such as the Maintenance Wizard that facilitates native SQL Server backups.

- **Analysis.** Data is valuable only when it is transformed into information. SQL Server supports this function with a number of native tools including English queries using multidimensional expressions (MDXs) and online analytical processing (OLAP) analysis that facilitates sophisticated analysis on large volumes of data. Specific to Microsoft Solution for Internet Business, SQL Server analysis is the foundation of the Microsoft Commerce Server 2000 Business Analytics function.

Commerce Server

Commerce Server plays a prominent role in the management and deployment of Web sites. It provides features and functions needed by all Web sites: the ability to know who visits your site, the ability to target content to visitors based on profile and context information, and the ability to understand what people are doing on your site so you can improve it. In Microsoft Solution for Internet Business, it provides the critical e-commerce platform needed to build an effective online business. This occurs with the Profile, Targeting,

Product Catalog, and Business Process Pipeline systems plus the following tools and capabilities:

- **Authentication.** A Commerce Server resource with global-level properties that is used to configure authentication options for a site.

- **User profiling and management.** A user profile is a set of predefined properties that describe a user (name, address, and other properties).

- **Expression.** A condition that is evaluated against user profiles to determine whether to deliver content or to perform another action. For example, an expression might be *user.totalvisit>100*. If this expression evaluates to TRUE, a specific piece of content is displayed.

- **Expression Builder.** This tool builds expressions. Expression Builder includes a list of common expressions from which you can define the properties you want to target. You can also use Expression Builder when creating a new target expression or catalog from the Campaign Expressions module.

- **Direct Mailer database.** A SQL Server database that contains e-mail messages, event data, and job data. This allows you to send personalized or nonpersonalized e-mail messages to large groups of people. Commerce Server Setup installs the Direct Mailer database when you install Commerce Server Direct Mailer. The database is installed on the same computer as Direct Mailer.

- **Packaging/Unpackaging.** Commerce Server Site Packager is a deployment tool that you use to package your site, applications, and resources into a single file (with a .pup extension) that you can then move to another computer.

- **Commerce Server Manager.** A system administration tool that you use to manage and configure Commerce Server resources, sites, applications, and Web servers.

- **Commerce Server Business Desk.** A Web-based site management tool available in Commerce Server 2000 that hosts business management modules you use to manage and analyze your e-commerce sites. This is accessible from any computer running Microsoft Internet Explorer 5.5 or later.

- **Product and service management (Retail Extension version only).** This allows you to present products and services in an intuitive way that allows customers to easily locate them along with related information.

- **Transaction processing (Retail Extension version only).** This includes electronic payment processing and an easy-to-perform checkout process that minimizes user input by using techniques such as stored profile information.

Note that Microsoft Solution for Internet Business uses Commerce Server for critical support for its different out-of-the-box deployments. However, traditional Internet development using Commerce Server is enhanced by the comprehensive software development kit (SDK) and administrative tools.

Microsoft Content Management Server

Microsoft Content Management Server is the enterprise Web content management system that enables companies to quickly and efficiently build, deploy, and maintain highly dynamic Internet, intranet, and extranet Web sites. Its capabilities can be divided into three areas: managing content, delivering content, and rapid development. Collectively, this all adds up to Content Management Server managing the content workflow: delivering content to a variety of places anytime, anywhere, including Web sites, databases, and devices.

Managing Content

Authoring templates that allow contributors to easily provide rich-formatted content support this area. This is a central paradigm to Microsoft Solution for Internet Business's easy management capability. Tools such as content tracking and archiving and content scheduling greatly assist the contributors in properly managing the content. The extensible object properties allow for the creation of metadata properties on content objects.

Delivering Content

The rapid dissemination of content is a key objective of Content Management Server and is met in several ways:

- **Dynamic page assembly.** In real time and as requested by the Web server, pages are created and presented.

- **Presentation templates.** Presentation templates facilitate quick and cost-effective site redesigns. These templates control site design and layout. Furthermore, the dynamic template switching capabilities using the Publishing application programming interface (API) allow presentation templates to be switched on the fly, facilitating real-time page design and layout changes.

- **Separation of content from format.** With this capability, content is stored and managed separately from the presentation template. This effectively increases efficiency in presenting information, as the data is "poured" into the template to which it is presented.

- **Content approval process.** The content workflow process can be configured so that content is approved by the appropriate parties prior to dissemination. This step ensures the accuracy of the content.

Rapid Deployment and Development

The following capabilities facilitate the rapid deployment of Content Management Server and the maintenance of a rapid development environment:

- **Quick installation.** Content Management Server installs easily through simple installation wizards, but further postinstallation configuration is necessary.

- **Sample templates and Web sites.** Sample templates, Web sites, and customization code are included in the box. Microsoft Solution for Internet Business uses its accelerator sites for demonstration and rapid deployment purposes.

- **Flexible COM API.** Developers can build powerful content management applications and share content with other systems using the flexible Publishing API.

- **Template and Resource Galleries.** Templates and Web site resources are managed on the server through Template Galleries and Resource Galleries to ensure centralized control over corporate publishing and design standards.

- **Dynamic site map.** Site map and navigation are generated automatically as pages are published to the site.

- **Site Deployment Manager.** This allows site administrators to easily move content and Web sites between servers.

- **XML.** Templates that publish content in XML format can be built easily.

Internet Security and Acceleration Server

Microsoft's third-generation firewall and caching server solution is Microsoft Internet Security and Acceleration Server 2000 (ISA). On the one hand, this is an effective software-based firewall solution that runs on a server machine running Windows 2000 Server. It supports network address translation, dynamic port filtering, and rules-based Internet access management. Sophisticated implementations are possible in which arrays of ISA servers can enhance performance and be used to design demilitarized zones (DMZs) that allow external access to approved Web sites but protect the internal corporate network.

Furthermore, ISA provides a highly regarded caching capability. Frequently accessed Web sites are cached on the server's hard disk for rapid retrieval at local area network (LAN) speed. This capability also allows you to effectively access these Web sites when your Internet connection fails.

BizTalk Server

BizTalk Server's key value is as an enterprise application integration tool. It is used for integrating back-end applications, both internal and external. This application facilitates the development and deployment of business rules and processes in an organization. It is often used to facilitate the interaction between trading partners in a transaction environment. The business processes are built and deployed with a visual tool called BizTalk Orchestration Designer. XML schemas are generated with the BizTalk Editor. BizTalk Messaging Manager automates the process of setting up trading profiles and agreements to exchange business documents over the Internet in a reliable and secure manner. Technically speaking, BizTalk supports Electronic Data Interchange (EDI), HTTP, HTTPS, Simple Mail Transfer Protocol (SMTP), and networked file shares.

BizTalk Adapters provide the key to enhanced interoperability with a wide variety of applications and technologies. Microsoft, along with a number of adapter development partners and application vendor partners, has built an impressive catalog of more than 140 adapters that reduce the effort required to integrate business processes.

Application Center

Application Center is Microsoft's deployment and management tool for high-availability Web applications. At its core, this tool reduces the complexity of managing large-scale Web sites with the following features:

- Scalability features allow this Microsoft Solution for Internet Business infrastructure to grow as your business grows.

- Several servers are treated as one server, including assistance with deployment over clusters.

- You can create logical groupings of application content, configuration, and components.

- Quality control is enhanced by life-cycle testing and deployment tasks.

- Network load balancing allows the efficient use of Web server resources.

- Health and performance monitoring is performed to proactively alert administrators to problems.

General Hardware Requirements

The hardware requirements for Microsoft Solution for Internet Business are appropriate, given the application support required. Considering the cost of hardware today, these requirements are well within financial reach for medium and large organizations. For server-side requirements, refer to the specific components (such as Microsoft SQL Server) that run on individual servers.

Client-side hardware requirements for the Business Desk or the Site Builder clients are well within reasonable guidelines and require an Intel Pentium II or higher compatible CPU, 128 MB of RAM, and at least 20 MB of free hard disk space.

You should check the Microsoft Solution for Internet Business Web site at *www.microsoft.com/solutions/msib* for updates to the hardware requirements.

Specific Microsoft Solution for Internet Business Solutions

There are several specific types of solution Web sites available for immediate deployment, as discussed in the following sections.

Corporate Web Sites

Corporate Internet sites are used for disseminating information about the company, its products, news releases, contact information, and so on. A corporate Web site built with Microsoft Solution for Internet Business will have the following features:

- **Intuitive navigation.** Users can quickly and easily locate information on your Web site.

- **Personalization.** You can deliver content to users based on information collected on the Web site about their behavior when they visited your site.

- **Fresh content.** You can update content without the involvement of technical staff. The content approval workflow ensures that content is approved before it is added to the site, and content can be scheduled for deployment.

Online Retail Sites

Online business-to-consumer (B2C) sites can import and update product catalogs, advertise, offer promotions, and process transactions. An online retail site built with Microsoft Solution for Internet Business has the following features:

- **Product presentation.** Products are presented in an intuitive way that allows customers to easily locate them along with related information.

- **Profile information.** Data describing site users is stored as a means of providing more relevant information to returning users, thereby enhancing revenue. This includes merchandising and promotion for products and services.

- **Personalization.** Content is presented dynamically to users based on profile information or contextual information such as time of day or current site location.

- **Transaction support.** An easy-to-perform checkout process minimizes user input using techniques such as stored profile information.

- **Content management support.** You can manage and update content, products, users, catalogs, orders, and site look and feel easily without technical support.

Government and Education Portals

Governments and educational institutions can easily communicate a wealth of information to their various constituencies through a Microsoft Solution for

Internet Business portal site. A government or education portal site built with Microsoft Solution for Internet Business can have the following features:

- **Content management support.** You can manage and update content, products, users, catalogs, orders, and site look and feel easily without technical support.

- **Approval process.** Content can be approved before it is deployed as a separate operation from content creation.

- **Personalization.** You can target personalized content to citizens, students, businesses, other governments, or employees based on user profiles.

- **Ability to contact interest groups.** You can deliver personalized, more relevant e-mail to citizens, students, businesses, other governments, or employees based on lists of users with similar interests or profiles.

Services

The next S of the Microsoft Solution for Internet Business solution is services. The Microsoft Solution for Internet Business services component is comprised of three service providers: certified partners, global system integrators, and MCS.

Certified Partners

First and foremost, Microsoft relies on its Microsoft Certified Gold Partners in the Microsoft Solution for Internet Business niche to assist customers in Microsoft Solution for Internet Business solution planning, deployment, and administration. Not only have these gold partners met the generic MCP standard of having a sufficient number of Microsoft Certified Professionals on staff, but these firms have also satisfied additional criteria to earn the "Gold Partner" designation.

For more information about MCPs, see *www.microsoft.com/partner*. Also visit the Microsoft Solution for Internet Business site at *www.microsoft.com/solutions/msib* for complete information on partners (such as which partner works the best for you).

Global System Integrators

Several large consulting firms, discussed on the Microsoft Solution for Internet Business site at *www.microsoft.com/solutions/msib,* are prepared to assist you in the planning, deployment, and administration of your Microsoft Solution for Internet Business site. These global system integrators have worked closely with the Microsoft Solution for Internet Business team to develop Microsoft Solution for Internet Business–specific niche expertise. Global system integrators have also attended the required Microsoft Solution for Internet Business course and passed the corresponding certification exam.

Microsoft Consulting Services

Some large customers already have a consulting relationship with MCS. MCS is in the business of providing enterprise-level planning consulting services to large customers. However, MCS typically brings in a certified partner to assist in the actual deployment and ongoing administration of a Microsoft solution such as Microsoft Solution for Internet Business. Consider using one of the Microsoft Technology Centers (MTCs) to plan and test the deployment of your Microsoft Solution for Internet Business site. These centers are part of MCS. For more information about MTCs, go to *http://www.microsoft.com/business/ services/mtc.asp* and pay special attention to the Microsoft Solution for Internet Business workshops and kickstart program. One MTC is discussed in the Appendix of this text. For more information about MCS, see *www.microsoft.com/business/services/mcs.asp.*

Support

Microsoft Solution for Internet Business customers benefit long after the solution has been deployed, with two support options that go beyond normal support mechanisms. This recognizes that Microsoft Solution for Internet Business customers need rapid, enterprise-level response. The two support levels, MSO-Level B and MSO-Custom, extend premier support with additional incident hours and fast response time guarantees (for example, one hour for emergencies). Table 10-1 lists the different levels of Microsoft's postsales support for Microsoft Solution for Internet Business.

Table 10-1. Levels of Postsales Support for Microsoft Solution for Internet Business

Service Type	Service Area	MSO-Level B	MSO-Custom
Prescriptive services	Service level agreement	✓	✓
	Solution custom code quick fix engineering (QFE) support	✓	✓
	Source code control	✓	✓
	Scalability and benchmarking labs	✓	✓
	Technical workshops	✓	✓
	Architectural review	✓	✓
Relationship and service level management	Solutions operational assessment	Additional fee	✓
	Account reporting	✓	✓
	Escalation contact	Named	On-site
	On-site advisory	✓	✓
	Solution workshops	✓	✓
Advisory services	Solution advisory services (setup, configuration, and operations)	✓	✓
	Solution QFE support	✓	✓
Resolution services	Rapid on-site support service	✓	✓
	Emergency break fix support (1 business hour)	✓	✓
	Critical break fix support (2 business hours)	✓	✓

(continued)

Table 10-1.   Levels of Postsales Support for Microsoft Solution for Internet Business   *(continued)*

	Standard break fix support (4 business hours)	✓	✓
	Pooled hours	800 hours	Custom hours
Internet and information services	Solution expert roundtables	✓	✓
	Solution news flashes	✓	✓

The benefits for Microsoft Solution for Internet Business customers include having a single support contact, enjoying a faster response time, and dealing with support professionals that are trained on the entire Microsoft Solution for Internet Business solution, not just the individual applications.

Solution Summary

With the Microsoft Solution for Internet Business components already defined in detail, this section brings it all together at a higher level. First, the capabilities of a Microsoft Solution for Internet Business site are succinctly presented. The next section provides a look at typical Microsoft Solution for Internet Business customer groups. Key Microsoft Solution for Internet Business features are listed next, and then Microsoft Solution for Internet Business market segmentation is discussed.

Capabilities of a Microsoft Solution for Internet Business Site

The following are representative of common characteristics of a Microsoft Solution for Internet Business site:

- **Analyzing site data.** You can run reports to analyze user data collected on your site.

- **Application integration.** You can integrate Microsoft Solution for Internet Business with back-end functionality.

- **Deliver personalized content.** You can deliver personalized content to anonymous and registered users based on data collected on your site.

- **Deliver targeted campaigns.** You can target campaigns to users based on data collected on your site.

- **Display products.** You can add, remove, and update products in your site catalog and create personalized catalogs.

- **Internationalization support.** You can present content in multiple languages with multiple currencies.

- **Manage content.** You can control the deployment of new content on your site by setting up a content approval workflow and scheduling deployment.

- **Manage transactions.** You can process purchases and manage orders easily.

- **Modular architecture.** You can easily add a variety of functions such as support for customer relationship management (CRM), sales and marketing, and e-commerce applications.

- **Publish content.** You can enable contributors to provide content that can be easily deployed on your site.

- **Scalability and robustness.** You can easily grow your Web site to accommodate increasing traffic.

- **Search functionality.** You can help your users locate information easily.

- **Site updates.** You can easily update the look and feel of your site by replacing logo graphics and other items throughout your site.

The preceding discussion can be summarized and viewed in the production deployment diagram shown in Figure 10-2. This figure is also useful in understanding the key features of Microsoft Solution for Internet Business, which are discussed later.

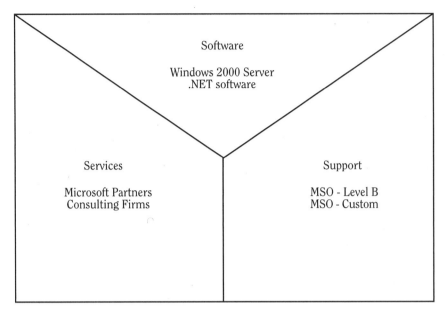

Figure 10-2. *Microsoft Solution for Internet Business production deployment diagram.*

Customer Groups

There are two Microsoft Solution for Internet Business constituencies: business users and technology users. Business users include the following:

- **BDMs.** These individuals are responsible for determining Microsoft Solution for Internet Business project scope and required investments that meet business needs. These individuals look to Microsoft Solution for Internet Business to empower employees to manage the Web technology, and they use Microsoft Solution for Internet Business's rich analytics for a 360-degree view of the business. This group faces challenges such as not being able to realize new business opportunities, not understanding customer behaviors, hearing feedback that users are having poor experiences on the company Web site, and concerns about weakened business/partner relationships. With a Microsoft Solution for Internet Business site, this group can realize new business opportunities, create more effective marketing strategies, be satisfied that users are having a positive experience on the company Web site, and build improved customer and partner loyalty.

- **Business managers.** These users are expected to interact with the Microsoft Solution for Internet Business site and make contributions (such as a marketing manager responsible for an advertising campaign).

- **Content creators.** Still part of the business users group, these are users who create content that appears on the site.

There are four types of technology users, also known as technical decision makers (TDMs):

- **Management.** Technology management individuals include chief information officers, directors of technology, and vice presidents of technology.

- **System architects.** These individuals provide the infrastructure and software blueprint.

- **Software developers.** These individuals write, test, and manage code and scripts.

- **System administrators and operators.** These individuals manage and monitor the server environment to maximize uptime and performance.

Key Features of Microsoft Solution for Internet Business

The key features of Microsoft Solution for Internet Business are described in the following sections.

Business Desk

Commerce Server Business Desk is an extensible tool that business managers use to manage and analyze their Web sites. Business Desk features can be used to update pricing information in catalogs, target new advertisements to specific users, and run reports to measure how these changes affect site productivity.

Personalization and Targeting

Personalization and targeting describe the processes of delivering personalized content to one or more users, or to any other business entity that has a profile. Microsoft Solution for Internet Business provides a high-performance, versatile platform that business managers can use to target content to any business-related item or condition. This capability lets companies engage in more effective merchandising and promotions based on customer profiles and behaviors.

Content Management

By empowering staff members with the comprehensive applications they need to manage their own content, enterprises benefit through increased productivity, stronger customer and partner relationships, improved internal communication, and increased revenue.

Content Workflow

A workflow and approval process built into Microsoft Solution for Internet Business ensures that content is always accurate. The business manager establishes workflow rules to implement a review and approval process.

Content Creation

Content creators can use the tool of their choice. Microsoft Content Management Server 2000 allows content creators to own their content. They no longer have to rely on cycles from the Web team every time they need to make a change or correction.

Analytics

The Commerce Server 2000 Business Analytics system provides business managers with advanced decision support using the Business Analytics system, which incorporates click-stream, user profile, product, campaign, and segmentation data.

Infrastructure Management

The Microsoft Solution for Internet Business solution provides the following infrastructure management tools:

- **Security.** Microsoft Windows 2000 provides numerous security features. ISA can provide additional firewall security.

- **Availability.** Windows .NET Enterprise servers provide high availability.

- **Manageability.** Site management is supported in Commerce Server Manager (a Microsoft Management Console snap-in) and Microsoft Application Center 2000.

- **Extensibility.** The .NET platform enables agile business management.

- **Supportability.** The Microsoft Solution for Internet Business solution includes a support plan designed to give you worry-free operation.

- **Scalability.** As your business successfully grows, Microsoft Solution for Internet Business is designed to scale upward and grow with you. This also includes performance enhancements such as network load balancing.

Site Management

Microsoft Content Management Server 2000 has extensive site management features that make Web sites built with it cost-effective to deploy and maintain. These features include the following:

- Centralized remote administration

- Archiving

- Integrated user administration

- Enterprise scalability

Market Segmentation

Basically it is customer complexity, not necessarily organizational size, that determines market segmentation. Microsoft Solution for Internet Business speaks to two market segments: large and medium.

Large Internet Presence

Characteristics such as heavy traffic and support for a variety of users are two characteristics of a large Internet presence. This segment utilizes all Microsoft Solution for Internet Business features to meet critical requirements in building the Web site. These businesses are utilizing Web technologies to more effectively run their businesses and include members of the Global 2000, online retail sites, and organizations with a dynamic Internet presence (corporate, government, and education).

The following are the key functionality requirements that characterize a large Internet presence:

- Heavy user traffic is supported by a scalable, reliable, and secure Web presence.

- Modular architecture is used to support and perform functions such as CRM, sales and marketing, and e-commerce applications.

- Content management capabilities allow you to manage, publish, and refresh content quickly and easily.

- Customers are allowed to personalize their Web sites, create a unique Web experience, and meet the goals of available information anytime, anywhere. This is the personalization function.

- Analytics that understand customer behaviors, anticipate needs, and measure the effectiveness of marketing campaigns are in place.

- Applications are integrated with back-end systems.

- Localization addresses the language needs of diverse customer groups.

- Search capabilities, including Web crawling, are provided.

Medium Internet Presence

Smaller in scale and scope, the company with a medium Internet presence typically displays the following characteristics:

- It has basic CRM and e-commerce functionality (for example, the retail transactional capability might be facilitated by a partner).

- It has click-stream analysis to measure the effectiveness of the Web presence.

- The ability to manage, publish, and refresh content is available.

- The site will have limited globalization and localization capabilities.

- Partners and vendors provide additional e-commerce capabilities.

- Not all Microsoft Solution for Internet Business capabilities are used.

Summary

This chapter described Microsoft Solution for Internet Business in an appropriate level of detail for the BDM. Two Microsoft Solution for Internet Business solutions exist: the baseline version and the Retail Extension version. Microsoft Solution for Internet Business is really comprised of four components: software, PAG, service, and support. Each of the components was reviewed in the chapter, including the individual software applications that comprise Microsoft Solution for Internet Business. In the next chapter, we take a look at the future of Internet business solutions.

The Future

Surprisingly, predicting the future of the Internet and its role isn't as hard as it seems. The natural maturation of the Internet sector closely follows that of more traditional business sectors. Business cycles exist and there is a trend toward consolidation. This mirrors the history of business dating back to the manufacturing era and perhaps even agrarian societies. Now the smart money is investing in and building Internet solutions for many of the reasons stated in this book, including better customer service and competitive repositioning.

This chapter, the final one in the book, is dedicated to looking forward based on the Internet solution foundation that you now have. The fundamentals of economic activity that will likely affect Internet solutions are presented. Proof of the Internet sector's strength, as provided by a variety of studies, is entered into evidence. The future of Internet solutions is discussed, including ways to build today and retain the value of an Internet solution tomorrow. Internet solutions from Microsoft are here for today and for tomorrow, evolving as your technology and business practices do.

Economics 101

Until someone proves otherwise, certain economic fundamentals will continue to influence the technology sector as a whole and the Internet solution area specifically. These include the declining costs of hardware, the increasing costs of technology labor, the shift in the supply curve due to a change in technology, customer expectation management, and barriers to entry. Each of these is discussed in this section.

Declining Costs

This section discusses Moore's Law relating to processing power and deployment, maintenance, and performance-related cost factors.

Moore's Law

Moore's Law, whereby the former Intel Corporation chairman predicted that processing power will double every 18 months, resulting in lower hardware costs, has stood the test of time. This is expected to be the case in the future as well, with several ramifications. Because the declining costs of hardware have neutralized the playing field for entrants seeking to deploy Internet solutions, it's a safe bet that more firms will develop and deploy Internet solutions. When applicable, such as in the retail sector, this will disenfranchise firms from their customers if they don't develop and deploy a capable Internet solution.

Deployment, Maintenance, and Performance

There is also a trend of lower technology solution deployment and maintenance costs because solutions, such as current Microsoft Internet solutions, are faster to deploy than competing and predecessor Internet business solutions. Internet solution setups are structured and integrated, removing some of the risk of failure in setting up first-generation Internet solutions. Today, this occurs in part by the Internet solutions prescriptive guidance, which helps customers quickly deploy Internet sites by filling the gap between traditional product documentation and knowledge about how to deploy the solution. Part of Microsoft's Internet solution implementation approach is also about integrating with custom solutions. Microsoft provides guidance on platform upgrade procedures in combination with other Microsoft solutions and with the customer's custom solutions.

Another case for declining costs centers on how Microsoft-based Internet solutions can easily be updated and maintained, which falls into the area of content management support. This is the ability to update content, products, users, catalogs, orders, and site look and feel easily without technical support. The operational procedures today are made more efficient by Microsoft's best practices in operating and securing a site, including site backup and firewalls. For example, Microsoft Support Options (MSO) Level B and Custom support options provide emergency and critical response times that are measured in minutes. This solution support provides you assured testing of service packs and hot fixes to meet your specific solution needs, plus on-site visits, guidance, access to resources dedicated to the solution, and proactive guidance on upcoming releases.

Increased reliability also factors into the declining costs argument. Microsoft Internet solutions are built on the reliable Microsoft .NET

Enterprise Servers, which in turn are configured to enterprise-scale requirements. This solution is a configuration of .NET Enterprise Servers that have been tested in world-class sites. Microsoft's Internet solutions have been tested and validated in configurations similar to those used by many corporate, government, and educational customers around the world.

All told, this points toward a declining cost curve for implementing Microsoft Internet solutions specifically and technology solutions in general.

Increasing Costs

As a general rule, labor costs are much "stickier" than other costs, with a tendency to ratchet upward. Whereas hardware costs have a history of declining, that is not the case with labor. This is a result of scarcity and customs. Scarcity is the initial primary driver for labor costs in the technology sector. Those with a skill set in high demand, such as leading-edge Internet technical skills, command high prices for their services. Rarely do skilled technical workers agree to a pay cut, thus the "sticky" nature of labor costs. Another factor is business practices and customs. A technology worker hired at $60,000 per year is typically retained by the firm even after the Internet solution deployment is complete and the easier maintenance phase period commences, although this work could be performed by a lower cost employee. Compounding the increasing cost argument for labor is the fact that this same worker, initially earning $60,000, will receive periodic cost-of-living and merit pay increases.

All told, these factors have contributed to a technology environment in which labor costs are on an increasing cost curve. This is expected to continue into the future.

Supply Curve Shift

The phenomenon of a shifting supply curve caused by changes in technology shows every sign of continuing in the future. Here's what this means: A retailer can provide 100 units of its product for $10 each using traditional sales and delivery methods (for example, a store with electronic cash registers). This firm then implements an Internet solution and becomes much more efficient. For example, assume this firm lowers its transaction costs and can now sell its product for $9 for each unit. This lower price to the customer is a result of the firm becoming more efficient because of a change in technology and a shift in the supply curve. This is shown in Figure 11-1.

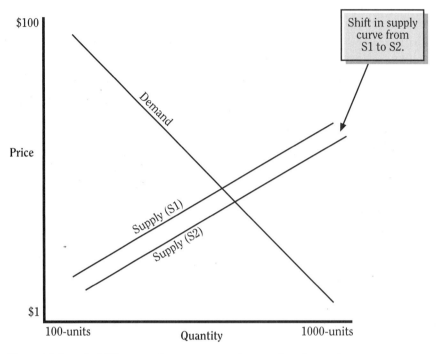

Figure 11-1. *A shifting supply curve means lower prices for customers.*

This example addresses a firm from a micro-economic perspective. However, shifting supply curves can also be viewed from a macro-economic perspective. Here, technology changes can benefit an entire firm; that is, the supply curve shift is on an aggregate basis. Examples of this include the introduction of a more efficient Internet solution in the future that is so compelling that the entire industry flocks to it. This hypothetical Internet solution lowers costs for all firms and these costs are passed on to the customer.

Customer Expectation Management

In economics, markets ebb and flow based on expectations. This is seen daily in the securities markets, and all other markets are subject to this same behavior. For example, if a firm believes that favorable economic conditions will exist in the future, it might elect to implement an Internet solution immediately, believing that this customer sales mechanism will allow it to sell more goods and thus reap profit.

Likewise, customers have expectations. Customers might expect their favorite retailer to have an Internet solution in place to conduct transactions at virtually any time, anywhere. The same retailer's Internet solution could also present information in a clear, personalized manner to make the customer feel unique. In the absence of such a solution, the customer might either defer purchases until such a solution is in place or shop elsewhere.

Barriers to Entry

There are two sides to the argument about the economic concept of barriers to entry. First, there is the digital divide argument between "haves" and "have nots" that such barriers exist when it comes to Internet solutions and will continue to exist in the future. The haves have the economic resources and know-how to implement an Internet solution and enjoy a competitive advantage in the marketplace. The have nots have neither the financial resources nor the know-how to implement effective Internet solutions and they fall further and further behind their competitors. A slight twist on this last point is that, lacking financial resources or know-how, new firms might not enter a direct retail space that depends on an Internet solution, thus effectively impeding this firm by a barrier to entry.

Second, there is a compelling case that Internet solutions have effectively lowered the barriers to entry in the marketplace. This is the "start an Internet-based company in your garage and become the next billionaire" argument. With hardware costs at historic lows and Internet solutions that are easy and inexpensive to implement and maintain, one could walk away believing that anyone with a few computers networked together with a fast Internet connection could become an Internet retailer. Of course, it is not as easy as it sounds, but the point is that many people believe that Internet solutions are empowering and will help launch more business in the future than they block. That is, current Microsoft Internet solutions and successor solutions in the future have effectively lowered the barriers to entry, not raised them.

The point here is not to necessarily take sides in the barriers to entry argument, but rather present both sides. As the business decision maker (BDM), you'll need to decide where you land on the barrier to entry debate and how it affects you. An Internet solution not only could let you enter new markets and attract new customers, but it might empower your employees in ways not previously possible, allow you to make more effective marketing decisions, better understand your customers, and enhance customer loyalty.

Proof Positive

As the famous adage goes, "Announcements of my death are premature." Such is the case in the early twenty-first century in the Internet economy hangover era. Bombarded by tightening economic conditions, true dot-com firms suffered a high failure rate, effectively downgrading the expectation of anything and everything related to the Internet. However, as this section shows, there is truly an expectation mismatch between the perceived shortfalls of Internet-related solutions and the facts, showing surprising support for e-commerce (of course based on Internet solutions). The Internet is a vital business channel that has already proven itself as a great communications vehicle. Regardless of the swaying winds of public opinion, many businesses are finding that Internet solutions can help distinguish themselves in business.

In the spirit of fair use, only snippets of some excellent studies are presented. At the end of the chapter, contact information is provided should you want to contact the research firms and acquire the complete studies to learn more about the Internet sector and the role of Internet solutions.

META Group

Two electronic business studies from META Group fuel the fire that Internet solutions not only are here to stay but also are poised to grow significantly in terms of implementations.

Content Management

In the report "Content Management: Part I—The Market" dated May 19, 2000, META Group found that, "By 2003, 95% of the G2000 will deploy XML-based content management infrastructures—often integrating document management, media asset management, imaging and electronic output management—to support anonymous authoring, application publishing, and dynamic virtual folders (data extraction, dynamic assembly, process automation, format translation, repository services, rights management, federated search, personalization, etc.) across the Internet, extranet, and intranet venues."

Those encouraging words were further compounded by an interesting observation that the Internet solutions industry, as a growing and viable sector, will experience consolidation in the future, making it incumbent on the BDM to bet on the right horse when selecting an Internet solution vendor.

Witness from the report: "As users and vendors increasingly recognize the importance of providing access to all relevant content for decision making, they will drive a $10B content management (CM) market by 2004 and further CM vendor consolidation prior to 2003. Beyond 2005, no more than five e-business keiretsus will dominate G2000 e-business technology."

It is expected that Microsoft will be among the five CM vendors just mentioned.

Commerce Chains

In the report of July 10, 2001 titled "Sailing Toward Next-Generation Commerce Chains," META Group proclaimed that, "Through 2004/05, G2000 organizations will concentrate e-business efforts on optimizing existing direct and indirect trading partner relationships (promoting chain wide advantages). Emphasis will be placed on driving channel efficiencies, collaborative planning, and selling. This will be accomplished by utilizing e-hubs, B2B sales/order processing and management facilities, and/or channel relationship management technologies."

Enough said.

IDC

The research firm IDC, in its 2001 bulletin titled "The Evolving eBusiness Web: B2B Market Model Forecast and Analysis, 2001 to 2005," by Richard Villars, found that the total worldwide value of goods and services purchased by businesses through e-commerce solutions will expand from $516 billion in 2001 to $4.3 trillion in 2005. The report states, "While this rise in commercial activity is impressive, innovation in information exchange between companies rather than basic e-commerce transactions will be much more important to long-term e-business success."

Gartner

Gartner presented news in its "Web Content Management and Portals: Who's Doing What?" report (L. Latham, July 30, 2001) that is music to the ears of BDMs. Gartner found that "Content management system prices will fall dramatically through 2004 (0.9 probability). Through 2004, portal prices will fall significantly, but not as much as prices for content management systems

(0.8 probability)." This finding affirms earlier statements in this chapter that the future of Internet solutions is one of lower costs in the context of hardware and software. This trend will benefit firms seeking to implement an Internet solution. Gartner also emphasized that Internet solutions customers should strongly consider focusing on top-tier providers to ensure technology continuity. Using a smaller firm's Internet solution might result in an "orphan" condition if the firm providing the Internet solution goes out of business.

Giga Information Group

Andrew Bartels, in his IDEABYTE paper titled "IT Trends: B2B and B2C E-Commerce" (July 18, 2001), found that 2001 to 2002 B2B sales through multiple e-channels (including electronic data interchange) would grow from $3.8 trillion to $4.4 trillion. Jane Stanhope, in her IDEABYTE paper titled "IT Trends: Commerce Servers" (July 19, 2001), predicted that between 2001 and 2002 (a 12-month analysis period), the following favorable trends would affect the Internet solutions area:

- There will be an ongoing migration from B2C to B2B and B2B2C.
- Value will remain the central focus in the Internet commerce realm.
- Although important, e-commerce will be just one of several corporate initiatives at the typical firm.
- Increased and more comprehensive commerce offerings can be expected.
- Larger e-commerce vendors will assert greater influence.

Contact Information

The following is the contact information to find out more about the studies referenced in this chapter.

META Group

208 Harbor Drive
P.O. Box 120061
Stamford, CT 06912-0061
203-973-6700
www.metagroup.com

Contact Information   *(continued)*

IDC

5 Speen Street
Framingham, MA 01701
508-872-8200
www.idc.com

Gartner

56 Top Gallant Road
Stamford, CT 06904
203-316-1111
www.gartner.com

Giga Information Group

139 Main Street
5th Floor
Cambridge, MA 02142
781-792-2600
www.gigaweb.com

Final Thoughts

In the hallowed halls of academia, legions of aspiring and eager MBAs have been taught that there is truly an attitude against starting, growing, and running a business in challenging times. The theory goes like this: in good times, it's relatively easy to be successful in business and you might be carried to profitability by the aggregate booming economy despite your individual business practices. This is the "it's easy to make money in good times" argument. Such positive conditions are forgiving when you make mistakes and don't strenuously test your management mettle. However, when times are less favorable, the true victors emerge. Those who truly know how to successfully run a business rise to the top, and others with less business acumen fall by the wayside.

Furthermore, there is more than sufficient anecdotal evidence that businesses started in challenging times are often more successful than those started in good times because the entrepreneurs who bravely move forward when others won't truly learn how to run lean, efficient, and smart organizations. If they fail, they are casualties of the marketplace. If they succeed, they have truly mastered what it takes to be a profitable entity.

Borrowing from Charles Dickens, the worst of times could also be the best of times. That is, when aggregate economic conditions suggest otherwise, it might be in your best interests to improve your operations with the introduction of new tools such as Microsoft Internet solutions. Not only could you enjoy an immediate competitive advantage in the marketplace with the introduction of such a capability, but in the future, when good economic times return, you'll have carved out precious market space at the expense of competitors that didn't invest in making their operations more efficient.

Microsoft Internet Solutions in the Future

As evolutionary solutions, Microsoft Internet solutions will enjoy the future enhancements described herein. Technologies, products, and services, as well as Microsoft's exciting new .NET initiative, will be incorporated into future versions of Microsoft Internet solutions. In a nutshell, it is important to understand that Microsoft Internet solutions will be actively updated to do the following:

- Take advantage of future advances such as new Microsoft .NET initiatives that exist only on the whiteboard today. This would include, but not be limited to, additional customer relationship management (CRM) capabilities.

- Increase the scope of guidance for data center and operational procedures.

- Provide prescriptive guidance for new Microsoft products and technologies in the context of the solution.

- Provide prescriptive guidance for integrating with other key line-of-business applications in our target customer scenarios.

Note that particular attention has been paid to investment preservation with Microsoft's Internet solutions. Because this solution is poised to take advantage of next-generation technologies, invest in Microsoft Internet solutions with the confidence that this solution will be able to grow as your business needs and the technology industry itself undergo changes.

.NET Advantages

Looking forward, Microsoft Internet solutions will continue to take advantage of .NET Enterprise Server generational improvements and product and service releases. This is consistent with Microsoft's stated viewpoint for .NET as realizing the next-generation Internet. Specifically, Microsoft looks to .NET to provide the following:

- **Data:** secure and universally accessible. Better interaction in a more secure way is a fundamental goal of the .NET initiative. Users will access data with traditional keyboard and mouse methods, but also with speech, handwriting, and vision technologies. Combined, the user will spend less time performing mechanical operations and more time being significantly more productive when performing tasks and accomplishing goals.

- **New applications, new services, and new development approaches.** The key point here is that XML is the backbone to the next generation of applications and services. Not only will the .NET building blocks change the way that applications can be developed, but they will enable the creation of whole new types of applications and services. These applications and services will blur the division between the Internet and operating systems, making the Internet itself the basis of the new operating system and new business opportunities for customers.

- **Beyond browsing, beyond dot-com.** Simply stated, in the future individual Web sites and devices connected to the Internet will strive to become an integrated whole. This is referred to at Microsoft as constellations of computers, devices, and services that work together to deliver broader, richer solutions. Microsoft .NET will help drive a transformation in the Internet that will see HTML-based presentations augmented by programmable XML-based information. Discussed in greater detail later, XML is a widely supported industry standard defined by the World Wide Web Consortium.

At the next level, the .NET core components are as follows:

- **.NET platform.** This includes four building blocks: Microsoft Visual Studio .NET, Microsoft .NET Enterprise Server, .NET Framework, and Microsoft Windows .NET. Visual Studio is the XML-based programming model and tools, fully supported by the Microsoft Developer

Network (MSDN) and .NET Enterprise Servers. The next generation of the Windows desktop platform, Windows .NET Server supports productivity, creativity, management, entertainment, and much more, and it is designed to put users in control of their digital lives. Tightly integrated with a core set of .NET building block services, it provides integrated support for digital media and collaboration, and can be personalized. It can also be programmed by .NET services, including MSN.NET, bCentral for .NET, and Microsoft Office .NET. Windows .NET Server will provide a rich platform for developers wanting to write .NET applications and services. Microsoft will also continue to offer and support versions of the Windows platform without .NET services.

- **.NET XML Web services.** The .NET XML Web services are a family of building block services, including Passport (for user authentication) and services for file storage, user preference management, calendar management, and many other functions. XML Web services allow applications to share data and invoke capabilities from other applications across any platform or operating system. Microsoft will offer many Web services in the future, as will a vast range of partners and developers who will also be able to produce corporate and vertical services built on the .NET platform.

- **Online services.** This includes the following specific services:

  - **Microsoft Network (MSN.NET).** By combining the leading content and services of MSN with the new .NET platform, MSN.NET will enable consumers to create a single digital personality and leverage smart services to ensure consistent, seamless, and safe access to the information, entertainment, and people they care about any time, any place, and on any device. Much of this functionality can already be seen at *www.msn.com,* where an individual can log on and enjoy e-mail, instant messaging, Passport-based authentication, and services such as MSN Money (an investment and money management service).

  - **Personal subscription services.** This includes new consumer-oriented services such as gaming.

  - **Office .NET.** These advanced communications and productivity tools—including universal canvas technology—combine communication, browsing, and document authoring into a single environment, enabling users to synthesize and interact with information in a unified way. Universal collaboration services will enable anyone to collaborate with people inside and outside their companies. A new architecture—based on smart clients and services—will provide rich functionality, performance, and automatic deployments on any device. Microsoft will also continue to offer and support versions of Office without .NET services.

- **Core building blocks.** The core Microsoft .NET building-block services that will be offered include the following:

    - **Identity.** Building on Microsoft Passport and Windows authentication technology, this service provides levels of authentication ranging from passwords and wallets to smart cards and biometric devices. It enables developers to build services that provide personalization and privacy for their customers, who in turn can enjoy new levels of safe and secure access to their services, no matter where they are or what device they are using.

    - **Notification and messaging.** This service brings together instant messaging, e-mail, fax, voice mail, and other forms of notification and messaging into a unified experience, delivered to any computer or smart device. This builds on the Hotmail Web-based e-mail service, Microsoft Exchange, and Instant Messenger.

    - **Personalization.** This service puts you in control by enabling you to create rules and preferences that implicitly and explicitly define how notifications and messages should be handled, how requests to share your data should be treated, and how your multiple devices should be coordinated (for example, always synchronize my laptop computer with the full contents of my Microsoft .NET storage service). It will also make moving your data to a new computer a snap.

    - **XML store.** This service uses a universal language (XML) and protocol (Simple Object Access Protocol [SOAP]) to describe what data means, enabling data to maintain its integrity when transmitted and handled by multiple Web sites and users. As a result, Web sites become flexible services that can interact and exchange and leverage each other's data. Microsoft .NET also offers a secure, addressable place to store data on the Web. Each of your devices can access this, optimally replicating data for efficiency and offline use. Other services can access your store with your consent. This service brings together elements of NTFS, Microsoft SQL Server, Exchange, and MSN Communities.

- **Calendar.** A crucial dimension of user control is time: when is it permissible to interrupt me, and when should I be left alone? This becomes especially important as people use more devices more often, and as users and services interact more richly. Microsoft .NET provides the basis for securely and privately integrating your work, social, and home calendars so that they are accessible to all of your devices and, with your consent, other services and individuals. This service builds on the Microsoft Outlook messaging and collaboration client and the Hotmail Calendar.

- **Directory and search.** Microsoft .NET makes it possible to find services and people with which to interact. Microsoft .NET directories are more than search engines or "yellow pages." They can interact programmatically with services to answer specific schema-based questions about the capabilities of those services. They can also be aggregated and customized by other services and combined with them.

New Microsoft Products

You will recall the discussion earlier in the chapter about expectation management. BDMs select paths and chart courses based on their expectations of the future. This is nothing new, and in fact, is the basis for most financial investments. To manage expectations, companies often communicate with the marketplace by signaling what the future holds. For example, in the case of financial investments, firms often issue a warning if they anticipate an earnings shortfall. In the case of technology, this type of signaling often comes from product announcements and speeches made at trade shows.

Microsoft, as the industry leader in software development, has communicated that its .NET suite is here for the long haul. You could say that Microsoft is, to borrow from Uniform Commercial Code (UCC) language, a "merchant in the trade" of software development. Microsoft is and will continue to be in the business of developing software solutions, including periodic upgrades to the .NET suite. Thus it is anticipated that the existing components used in Microsoft Internet solutions will not only be upgraded on a regular basis, say every 18 to 24 months, but that new components will be added as appropriate. As you might imagine, some of these components are on the drawing board already, poised for development. Other future components are not even imagined as of this writing, still awaiting discovery.

This discovery process, the research phase, enjoys significant support from Microsoft. If you look at the company's 2001 annual report, you see that the research and development (R&D) expense of $4.38 billion is the second greatest expense to Microsoft (exceeded only by sales and marketing at $4.88 billion). That is an astounding 17 percent of revenue. To add more meaning to this number, compare how it stacks up against the R&D spending undertaken by two other Internet solution developers. A leading database development firm, in its most recent financial statements for the year ending 2000 (this is comparable to the Microsoft figures, as the calendar dates vary only slightly), spent 10 percent of revenues on R&D. A leading mainframe hardware manufacturer and service provider, in its recent 10-Q statement filed with the Securities and Exchange Commission (SEC), shows that for the nine months ending September 30, 2001, its R&D spending (as measured in the research, development, and engineering category) was $3.7 billion, or only 5.9 percent of revenue.

Future investments in .NET are also summarized in the following passage excerpted from the Microsoft 2001 annual report letter from Bill Gates and Steve Ballmer:

"In addition to these major new product launches, Microsoft is laying a solid framework for the future with a projected investment of approximately $5 billion in research and development in fiscal 2002. At the center of our R&D efforts is Microsoft .NET, an innovative effort as significant in the development of computing as the graphical user interface and the introduction of the Internet. .NET is Microsoft's platform for a new computing model built around XML Web Services. Just as the Web revolutionized how users interact with content, XML is revolutionizing how applications communicate with data and how computers and devices communicate—by providing a universal data format that lets information be easily shared, adapted, or transformed. .NET will create new opportunities for Microsoft and for thousands of developers and industry partners by enabling constellations of PCs, servers, smart devices, and Internet-based services to collaborate seamlessly. Businesses will be able to integrate their processes, share data, and join forces to offer customers much more dynamic, personalized, and productive experiences— across the PC and an expanding universe of devices—than are available today."

With respect to specific Microsoft technologies and solutions, look for the ability to extend Microsoft Internet solutions by embracing future releases of Commerce Server, BizTalk Server, SQL Server, and the other .NET components.

Microsoft's other signal to the market regarding future product development is founder Bill Gates's job title as Chief Software Architect. Removed from the day-to-day management of Microsoft, Gates is free to focus on R&D

issues as well as existing products. This fact shouldn't be minimized in your quest to make the best possible technology decision with the facts and information available to you. Reading tea leaves is one thing, but respecting the company's stated commitment to R&D is entirely another when making this decision.

As a BDM, it is essential that you factor in not only what Microsoft Internet solutions can do for you today, but also what your expectations are for Microsoft Internet solutions when making your Internet solution decision. In other words, its important to take advanatage of today in an intelligent way with technologies that are committed to being there tomorrow.

Integration with Other Applications

This section relates to third-party .NET services. Behind this initiative stands a vast range of partners and developers who will have the opportunity to produce corporate and vertical services based on the .NET platform. This translates into opportunity for software developers who want the opportunity to create advanced new services for the Internet age. This includes services that are able to automatically access and leverage information either locally or remotely, working with any device or language, without having to rewrite code for each environment. As stated by Microsoft in its June 22, 2000 white paper titled "Microsoft .NET: Realizing the Next Generation Internet," "everything on the Internet becomes a potential building block for this new generation of services, while every application can be exposed as a service on the Internet."

Our prediction? Look for leading broad and narrow vertical market application vendors to exploit the .NET building blocks to deliver business information in ways that are faster and richer than imagined today. This will lead to the next wave of the Information Age revolution. Businesses that participate by implementing appropriate Internet solutions will emerge victorious in the context of e-commerce. That's a point made in this chapter and repeatedly throughout this book.

Your next step is to view more information about Microsoft Internet solutions at *www.microsoft.com/solutions/msib*. This will allow you to integrate some of these abstract comments with the current reality of Microsoft Internet solutions.

Summary

This capstone chapter integrated many of the salient points that surfaced between the pages of this book and provided a necessary and optimistic forward look. You learned early in the chapter that the Internet sector is subject to the economic laws of nature, not immune to them. In the late 1990s, it was all too easy to believe the Internet e-commerce bubble was somehow not subject to the laws of supply and demand, but the early twenty-first century proved otherwise. However, opportunities for sound business models always exist, irrespective of the broader general economy. Internet-based businesses with strong financial fundamentals can supplement that strength with Internet solutions from Microsoft. The underlying strength of the Internet sector was explored through the insights offered by several leading research houses and analysts. Predictions on the future of Microsoft Internet solutions were proffered with a recommendation that your next step be to peruse *www.microsoft.com/solutions/msib* for current information.

The JellyBelly.com Story

The Jelly Belly Candy Company faced a problem with its Web site. Its three-year-old shopping cart application was generating dissatisfaction from online customers, and as a result the company lost money because it was not able to take immediate advantage of customer demand. One of the chief complaints was the inability to designate multiple shipping addresses in a single site visit; instead, customers had to create separate shipping orders for each distinct address. "We were getting a lot of angry e-mail from our customers about this. Many of our customers wanted to send gifts for their family, friends, and co-workers in one trip, and the inability to designate multiple addresses meant they had to spend a lot more time ordering products. It was not a good user experience," said Ryan Schader, Director of Corporate Strategy.

Problems with the Site

The old shopping cart application was suitable for a low-volume Web site, but with its surging popularity Jelly Belly needed something new. The current site was running on an unsupported software platform and it just couldn't keep up. Prior to being replaced, the Web site application ran on a single Microsoft Windows NT server, and the application was quickly overwhelmed. The application crashed regularly, which translated into many hours of down time, which in turn meant that revenue wasn't being generated. In addition, the vendor was unable to keep up with software maintenance or requested feature updates, such as a multiple address book feature. The site was also slow to perform its basic function of online product ordering. The overall user experience was not a good one.

To be fair, the software vendor didn't have control over numerous variables, such as network design or data mining activities. However, it was apparent that Jelly Belly needed a change, and fast. "The site wasn't meeting our customers' needs, and it wasn't meeting our needs," said Schader. The decision was a simple one for Jelly Belly, but with important consequences for its Internet presence: fix the site, or remove it altogether.

The Business Case for Change

To make a case for fixing the site, Schader conducted a business analysis of his company's goals and current Web site performance. It quickly became clear that the data backed up the anecdotal evidence of customer e-mails: the site was significantly underperforming, resulting in dollars lost. "Clearly we were leaving money on the table," said Schader. Although online sales are not the lion's share of the company's revenue, the site was strategically important to Jelly Belly's image in the confectionary niche market. When the site performed poorly, Jelly Belly's image also suffered in the eyes of its customers, weakening the corporate brand. In the business-to-consumer realm, two goals were paramount: fix what was broken and improve the customer experience. Both goals could be easily measured using commonly available metrics: Increased uptime would translate directly into measurably increased revenue because of increased availability to customers for longer periods of time. An improved customer experience would be measured by both shorter time to complete an online order and the reduced numbers of customer complaints.

In addition, the team at Jelly Belly was looking to the future. Most of their business derives from sales to national retail chains, distributors, and gourmet candy retailers. The purchase order system at the time relied on older, more costly technology; faxes were by far the highest volume order method, followed by telephone orders, both of which were cost-intensive to process. Jelly Belly was looking to implement a catalog management system that would enable customized content and pricing for its multitiered customer base. The distribution chain would benefit by having real-time order entry and status updates, and Jelly Belly would benefit by gaining better business information about its customers and purchasing trends. The existing e-commerce platform could not be expanded to support these requirements.

One final consideration came into play during the business analysis phase. It became important to work with an end-to-end solution provider who could tackle all the issues likely to arise, from network design to application compatibility to hosting issues. "We're a candy company, not an e-commerce application development and managed services company," said Dan Rosman, Director of IT.

The Solution: The Microsoft Solution for Internet Business and the Microsoft Technology Center

The Microsoft Solution for Internet Business met the business and technical needs put forth by Jelly Belly. Microsoft, in partnership with Accenture, proposed an end-to-end solution that included network consulting, Web site hosting, catalog and application design, and a service level agreement for guaranteed uptime. Dedicated developers were assigned, and design and testing was performed at the Silicon Valley Microsoft Technology Center (MTC) in Mountain View, CA.

The technical strengths of Microsoft Solution for Internet Business enabled Jelly Belly to duplicate the functionality of the old solution and build in the multiple-address functionality in a short time span. They built dual Web servers, based on Microsoft Windows 2000 Advanced Server, hooked to clustered databases on the back end for redundancy, along with hardware failover at crucial points in the network. The basic ordering Web site was simple to deploy, but coding the multiple shipping address ability took additional work, testing, and debugging. When it was combined with the end-to-end solution, however, it meant that Jelly Belly had finally found a solution that met the business goals of increased uptime and improved end-user experience.

For Jelly Belly, it was a solution just in the nick of time. "The new site had to be online for the post-Thanksgiving Christmas rush, when most people do their gift shopping," said Schader. "In addition, Jelly Belly Candy Company has the U.S. rights to produce the Bertie Bott's jelly beans featured in the Harry Potter movie released in November, and we wanted to capitalize upon the visibility created by the movie. We had an incredibly aggressive timeline, and we were ready to roll close on the heels of the movie's release." He cautioned, though, that you should beware of vendors promising a plug-and-play solution. "You can't just take a software package, install it, and think you have an online catalog. The e-commerce environment is hostile; you need to understand the technology and have experience building these types of sites. While we didn't have that development experience up front, we knew what worked and what didn't, and that was a big help in working with Microsoft and Accenture."

Concluded Steve Lee, Business Development Director for the Silicon Valley MTC, "JellyBelly.com is a great project for Microsoft. The name recognition is international. The ability to facilitate and assist JellyBelly.com with a total solution that was value priced was even more satisfying than beating out the competition. JellyBelly.com was not only looking for a solution in the Microsoft Solution for Internet Business but a group and facility that was dedicated to its success in deployment as well as customer satisfaction. There are larger enterprises that we could have asked to be an early adopter of Microsoft Solution for Internet Business but none as fun and challenging as JellyBelly.com. When we bring VIPs to the MTC to tour our facilities, everyone wants to know more about JellyBelly.com and its gourmet jelly beans and its decision to commit to Microsoft for its B2C and B2B e-commerce platform and servers."

Glossary

Active Directory The directory service for Microsoft server operating systems starting with Windows 2000 Server. Active Directory stores information about objects on the network, such as user accounts. It is also a critical part of the network operating system security model, allowing users and other objects to access resources for which they have permissions.

Active Server Pages A server-side scripting environment that can be used to build dynamic Web sites, pages, or applications.

amortization The repayment of the principal amount of a loan in installments during the loan's life.

auditing Tracking users' activities by recording selected types of events in security logs.

authorization A process that verifies a user has the proper permissions to access a resource such as a Web site or database file.

availability A fault tolerance measure for a computer, such as a server-based networking environment.

book value The accounting value of an asset.

boundarylessness The idea that solutions to business problems should encompass everyone involved, whether inside or outside the formal borders of a corporation.

breakeven analysis An analytical technique for studying the relationship among fixed cost, variable cost, and profit.

business-to-business (B2B) site An e-commerce Web site designed for the creation and transmission of purchase orders between businesses.

business-to-consumer (B2C) site An e-commerce Web site designed for retail shopping by the public.

campaign A marketing program that uses many communication vehicles (for example, ads and direct mail) to accomplish a specific result, such as increasing market share or introducing new products.

capacity planning Planning for applications and hardware and network infrastructure requirements to support expected site traffic and to achieve site performance goals.

capital budgeting   The process of planning expenditures on assets whose returns are expected to extend beyond one year.

checkout   The process of finalizing a purchase or transaction on a Web site.

Commerce Server Business Desk   A Web-based site management tool in Commerce Server 2000 and its successors that provides business management modules you can use to manage and analyze your e-commerce sites.

cookie   A file that contains information about a user, including name, identification number, password, and click history.

cost of capital   The discount rate that should be used in the capital budgeting process or valuation computations.

cutoff point   The minimum rate of return on acceptable investment opportunities.

data mining   The process of identifying commercially useful patterns or relationships in databases or other computer repositories through the use of advanced statistical tools.

data store   A database file containing data used by an e-commerce site, such as registered user and product information.

data warehouse   A database that can access all of a company's information. While the warehouse can be distributed over several computers and can contain several databases and information from numerous sources in a variety of formats, it should be accessible to users through simple commands.

decision tree   A device for setting forth graphically the pattern of relationship between decisions and probability factors.

Digital Subscriber Line (DSL)   A regular twisted-pair telephone line that carries digital rather than analog signals, increasing the bandwidth of the line. Also known as ADSL.

e-commerce   The overall process of buying and selling goods, products, and services over the Internet.

electronic data interchange (EDI)   An electronic data transfer method between different companies. The network backbone used is typically a private wide area network or the Internet.

executive information system (EIS)   A set of tools designed to organize information into categories and reports for senior executives. Many EIS systems were difficult to integrate with other corporate information systems.

Today, EIS usually stands for Enterprise Information System and is designed to provide information to a wider range of people in an organization.

explicit profiling   An information gathering process whereby users visiting a Web site offer information about themselves, such as contact information (name, street, city, state, ZIP/Postal Code).

feedback loop   A system to gather reactions from customers about a product or service in order to create a continuous cycle of improvements, more feedback, and more improvements.

firewall   A security point that separates a private network from a public network. It is not uncommon to see organizations use multiple layers of firewalls.

frequently asked questions (FAQs)   Pronounced "facts," this is a common feature of Web sites that includes answers to common questions related to that site.

Gantt chart   A bar chart that shows individual parts of a project as bars against a horizontal time scale. Gantt charts are used as a project-planning tool for developing schedules.

goodwill   Intangible assets of a firm established by the excess of the price paid for the going concern over its book value.

groupware   Software that enables a group of users on a network to collaborate on a particular project. Groupware software supports common office functions such as e-mail, collaborative document development, scheduling, and tracking.

hit   A client computer request for an image or file from a Web server. Hits are a common measure of Web site popularity.

horizontal integration   A business model for the computer industry in which each layer of technology—chips, systems, software, solutions, and service—is provided by a different set of companies. Fierce competition in each area drives technology ahead rapidly and creates a high-volume, low-price model. *See also* vertical integration.

Hypertext Transfer Protocol (HTTP)   A protocol that facilitates client/server communication over the Internet, specifically Web sites.

implicit profiling   An information collection process in which the actions and behaviors of a user visiting a Web site are recorded.

independent software vendor (ISV)   A vendor that develops software, such as business productivity applications.

inflection point   In mathematics, the term that describes the point at which the shape of a curve shifts from concave to convex; in business, the term that describes a sudden and massive change in a business market or technology use. Popularized by Intel Chairman Andrew Grove.

information work   A phrase coined by MIT's Michael Dertouzos to describe the transformation of passive data into active information by human brains or software.

institutional intelligence, institutional IQ, corporate IQ   A measure of how easily a company can share information broadly and how well people within an organization can build on each other's ideas and learn from past experiences.

Internet   A disparate set of computer networks interconnected using the common TCP/IP protocol suite standard.

Internet domain name   An Internet site name that is registered with a domain name registration authority. The second-level domain name *Microsoft.com* is an Internet domain name.

Internet service provider (ISP)   A public carrier of remote access to the Internet. An ISP can host a Web page for a customer and provide additional services such as e-mail. Microsoft's MSN service is an ISP.

intranet   An internal network design for information technology. Typically an intranet is viewed in the context of internal Web sites, not just network infrastructure.

just-in-time   A system of inventory control based on the Japanese kanban system in which materials are delivered just in time for manufacturing. The better the information system between a company and suppliers, the less inventory the company has to stock and the lower its costs.

knowledge management   A concept that pertains to the use of information management technology to cultivate the accumulated expertise within an organization. This technology often provides features that bolster communication, coordination, and collaboration.

knowledge worker   Employee whose fundamental task is analyzing and manipulating information. PC systems can turn more employees into knowledge workers by giving them better information about the processes they are carrying out.

leverage factor   Ratio of debt to total assets or debt to equity.

liquidity   A firm's cash position and its ability to meet maturing obligations.

metadata or meta data   Broad data used to describe other data. Also known as "data about data."

migration   A transition from an older hardware platform, operating system, or software version to a newer one.

netiquette   The dos and don'ts of online communication. In the online world, which is devoid of subtle hints like inflection and body language, netiquette makes communication clearer and more precise. Netiquette examples include short titles, brief descriptions, and proper spelling.

operating system   This is the programming code that controls the basic operations of a computer and network, such as printing and logon security.

opportunity cost   The rate of return on the best alternative investment that is available. It is the highest rate of return that will not be earned if the funds are invested in a discrete, competing project.

payback period   The length of time required for the net revenues of an investment to return the cost of the investment.

personalization   This capability is used to direct Web-based content or e-mail messages to servers based on individual profile information.

pipeline   A software infrastructure that defines and links together one or more stages of a business process, running them in sequence to complete a task.

point-of-sale (POS)   The place in a store where goods are paid for. Computerized scanners for reading tags and bar codes, electronic cash registers, and other special devices record purchases. POS systems connected with digital analysis tools enable real-time analysis of sales and faster response to changing customer demand.

portfolio   Combining assets to reduce risk by diversification.

profile   A set of characteristics that define any business-related matter or item. This would include a user, company, or business process.

reengineering   The design of new business processes, usually in conjunction with digital systems, to improve corporate responsiveness to changing business conditions.

registered user   An individual who visits a Web site and provides personal information such as logon credentials, name, or e-mail address.

return on investment (ROI)   A financial performance measure of how well and efficiently an asset is functioning. For example, the ROI of a real estate investment is easily calculated by looking at the earnings returned by the investment.

risk   The degree of dispersion of future returns from their average expected value. Can be measured by standard deviation, variance, or coefficient of variation for future returns.

site   Typically denotes a collection of Web pages. Also, in Commerce Server Manager, this is a container for applications and other site-level resources. *See also* Web site.

skunkworks   Any small team that goes off by itself to develop a new product outside of a company's normal development processes. Named for the secret group at Lockheed that developed a number of high-technology aircraft.

task worker   Employee assigned to a single, repetitive task with little autonomy. Modern business principles encourage the use of technology to automate many tasks and redesign others to take advantage of a worker's skills.

time to market   The amount of time it takes a company to go from concept to initial shipment of a product.

total cost of ownership (TCO)   The cost of owning, operating, and maintaining a computer system. TCO includes the up-front costs of hardware and software plus the costs of installation, training, support, upgrades, and repairs. Industry initiatives designed to lower TCO include centralized network management of PCs, automated upgrades, and "self-healing" PCs.

trading partner   Two or more organizations that are trusted and exchange electronic data amongst themselves. The information is typically financial in nature.

user profile   A grouping of properties that describe a user, such as name, postal address, and e-mail address.

value network, Value Chain Initiative   A web of partnerships enabled by digital information flow so that a company and all its suppliers can easily communicate and act together. In a value network, everyone who touches the product—from retailer to distribution to transportation to manufacturing—must add value, and communications go both forward and backward among all companies involved.

vertical integration   An older business model for the computer industry in which most layers of technology—chips, systems, software, solutions, and service—were provided by a single vendor. Sales volumes were low, and switching costs for customers were high because every piece of the solution would have to change.

visit   A series of requests from a visitor or user at a Web site.

Web site   A collection of files, applications, and Web pages accessed via a Web address over the Internet.

Webcasting   The use of the Web to distribute news and information.

working capital   A firm's investment in short-term assets, such as cash, that can be used to finance current operations.

Index

Symbols and Numbers

101communications, 28–29

A

accelerator site, Microsoft Solution for Internet Business, 159
account profiles, 94
accounting practices, 53
acquisitions, system integration and, 12
Active Directory service, Microsoft Windows 2000 Advanced Server, 162
Application Center, Microsoft Solution for Internet Business, 168–69
application integration
    benefits of, 38–39
    BizTalk Server and, 168
    Microsoft Solution for Internet Business and, 174
application model, MSF, 110–11
applications
    architecture, 115
    development of, 47
    Windows 2000 Advanced Server, 162
architecture
    business architecture, 114–15
    information architecture, 116
    modular, 175
    services, 84
    structured, MOF, 124
    technology architecture, 116–17
assessment. *See* measurements and assessments
auditing, projects, 152
authentication
    Commerce Server and, 165
    .NET and, 193

B

B2B (business-to-business), 79, 188
B2C. *See* business-to-consumer
Ballmer, Steve, 195
barriers to entry, 185
Bartels, Andrew, 188
BDMs. *See* business decision makers
best practices, MRF, 103
BizTalk Server, 168
budgeting, 148–49
building phase, TCO model, 120
business analytics
    benefits of, 35

business analytics *(continued)*
    improving capabilities for, 11–12
    key performance indicators and, 80
    Microsoft Solution for Internet Business, 178
    overview of, 6
business architecture, 114–15
business decision makers (BDMs)
    barriers to entry and, 185
    characteristics of, 7
    customer-focused models and, 6
    as customers for Microsoft Internet solutions, 176
    project liaison with, 135
Business Desk, Commerce Server, 61, 165, 177
business goals. *See also* needs analysis
    aligning IT goals with, 103
    defining, 13
    pain analysis and, 16
    scope of, 13–14
    strategic planning, 14–15
business managers, 160, 177
business models, 3–4
business partners, 65. *See also* partners
business presence, extending via Internet, 9
business value, 59. *See also* return on investment (ROI)
business-to-business (B2B), 79, 188
business-to-consumer (B2C)
    communication, 79
    enhancements for, 71
    migration to B2B, 188
    sites, 170

C

101communications, 28–29
caching, 159
calendar, .NET, 194
cash inflows, ROI, 55
catalog management, 89–91
catalog sales, 89
CEOs (chief executive officers), 17, 89
CertCities.com, 28
certification, 140–41
certified partners, Microsoft, 171
CFOs (chief financial officers), 17
chain of command, 60–61
change management, 104
chief executive officers (CEOs), 17, 89
chief financial officers (CFOs), 17
chief technology officers (CTOs), 17, 89
class libraries, 159

Get a **Free**
e-mail newsletter, updates,
special offers, links to related books,
and more when you

register on line!

Register your Microsoft Press® title on our Web site and you'll get
a FREE subscription to our e-mail newsletter, *Microsoft Press Book
Connections.* You'll find out about newly released and upcoming books
and learning tools, online events, software downloads, special offers
and coupons for Microsoft Press customers, and information about
major Microsoft® product releases. You can also read useful additional
information about all the titles we publish, such as detailed book descriptions, tables of contents and indexes, sample chapters, links to
related books and book series, author biographies, and reviews by
other customers.

Registration is easy. Just visit this Web page and fill in your information:

http://www.microsoft.com/mspress/register

Microsoft®

- -

Proof of Purchase

Connecting to Customers
0-7356-1500-4

CUSTOMER NAME

Microsoft Press, PO Box 97017, Redmond, WA 98073-9830